T0304061

Wealth

This title, first published in 1920, is an excellent introduction to the fundamentals of economics, including explanations of production, distribution, and capital. Kirkaldy further highlights the economic problems of trade, commerce, exchanges, and finances. This title will be a valuable resource to students of Business and Economics, and is equally suitable for general readers interested in learning the basics of economics.

Wealth

A.W. Kirkaldy

Routledge
Taylor & Francis Group

First published in 1920
by Methuen & Co. Ltd

This edition first published in 2016 by Routledge
2 Park Square, Milton Park, Abingdon, Oxon, OX14 4RN
and by Routledge
711 Third Avenue, New York, NY 10017

Routledge is an imprint of the Taylor & Francis Group, an informa business

© 1920 Methuen & Co. Ltd

Publisher's Note
The publisher has gone to great lengths to ensure the quality of this
reprint but points out that some imperfections in the original copies may
be apparent.

Disclaimer
The publisher has made every effort to trace copyright holders and
welcomes correspondence from those they have been unable to contact.

A Library of Congress record exists under LC control number: 21003404

ISBN 13: 978-1-138-18796-2 (hbk)
ISBN 13: 978-1-315-64277-2 (ebk)

WEALTH
ITS PRODUCTION AND DISTRIBUTION

BY

A. W. KIRKALDY, M.A.

B.LITT. OXFORD, PROFESSOR OF ECONOMICS AND COMMERCE
UNIVERSITY COLLEGE, NOTTINGHAM

METHUEN & CO. LTD.
36 ESSEX STREET W.C.
LONDON

First Published in 1920

GENERAL EDITOR'S PREFACE

THIS book is designed to explain in a lucid and popular manner the fundamental facts in the *Production* of Wealth, and the causes which regulate its *Distribution*. It gives an analysis of the functions of *Nature*, of *Man*, and of *Capital* in the *Production* of Wealth ; and it traces the conditions upon which the economic progress of mankind depends. There is an abundance of illustration from various fields of industry, gathered both from study and the wide experience of the author and his intimate knowledge of practical affairs.

This subject is a necessary introduction to the further study of economic problems concerning Trade, Commerce, Exchanges, and Finance.

G. ARMITAGE SMITH.

CONTENTS

WEALTH
ITS PRODUCTION
AND DISTRIBUTION

I

INTRODUCTION

ECONOMICS has been looked upon as a science ever since Adam Smith, in 1776, published his enquiry into the causes of the wealth of nations. From that time, at any rate, there have been conscious economists in the world, but it would be a great mistake to suppose that economics came into being about the middle of the eighteenth century. The subject matter of economics is wealth, not, however, in the narrow sense understood by the man in the street, which is synonymous with abundance. The real economist is he who strives to get at the natural laws affecting man's material well-being, and is not necessarily engaged, as is sometimes erroneously thought, in trying to show how either an individual or a nation can become rich. From this point of view the task before the economic investigator is to unravel and make plain those natural laws—as old as humanity itself—which control the material side of life. If these laws be studied, noted, and observed, the individual or the community, acting in accordance with them, develops his or its well-being naturally. If, however, either an individual or a nation either ignores or acts in opposition to these laws there must result loss and inconvenience.

Thus at the outset of this short essay on the production and distribution of wealth it will not be amiss to devote a few pages to a consideration of how man became conscious that nature must be studied if he wished to be really successful in business and commerce ; or if as a group he aimed at developing a nation that should be materially well-balanced, harmonious, and contented.

Considered from the material side mankind has passed through four great stages of development.

In the first stage man was a hunter. He lived by the chase, and a very hard life it must have been. He had to " catch his hare before he could cook it " ; and when he faced the animal world equipped merely with his own hands he was at a serious disadvantage. But he must soon have learned the value of a stick or a stone to help him bring down some animal or bird. The first man who used an implement to assist him in gaining a meal little imagined that he was using capital for the first time, or that he had brought into use an instrument that was to ease the heavy burden of toil and make the development of the higher side of life a possibility. As a hunter man lived on the flesh of the victims to his skill, and he used the skin of animals as clothing.

The hunting stage was full of interesting economic problems, as fortunately can be seen by visiting those parts of the world where man still pursues the hunter's career.

How long hunting remained the great occupation for the great majority of mankind is a matter for speculation, but this stage gradually shaded off into a new era and mankind entered upon the pastoral period. How did man learn to become a shepherd or a dairyman ? The question is more easily answered by the imagination than by referring to historical records. Was it woman who first discovered that animals could be domesticated ? It may well be so. Probably some hunter had killed a she-goat and the kids refused to leave the dead mother. They were perhaps taken as pets, and on attaining maturity the utility of milk was discovered. However it originated man found out that certain animals could be tamed, and that in that condition they were of greater value than in the wild state. Man himself, too, began to develop new qualities, family life developed the kindly side of his nature, he desired a less uncertain means of existence, and the new possibility was tested and developed. In a word a new era opened, the pastoral stage was inaugurated. Not all at once, but gradually the hunter developed into the shepherd.

As a hunter man had no fixed abode, nor did he settle down as a shepherd. He wandered about with his flocks and herds seeking pastures new and the necessary water supply. Then he noted the qualities of certain grasses, shrubs, and trees. He found that by care and attention new qualities were developed in certain forms of vegetation. To benefit by these it was necessary to remain for a period in one spot, and so land settlement commenced. Gradually the advantages of farming became recognised, and man began to combine his care of animals with the cultivation of the land.

While these changes were taking place it became plain that some men were more skilled in certain occupations than in others. One man could hunt or fish or kill animals more skilfully than another. The making of primitive tools, weapons, and clothes also lent itself to this same phenomenon. In the manufacture of flint arrow-heads or axes one man excelled. He could produce not only a more satisfactory weapon than another man, but in less time. The practice of separate occupations was seen to be an advantage, and with this, exchange commenced. The secret of exchange is the possessing of a surplus that is not required for one's own use. The successful maker of flint tools and weapons was possibly only an indifferent hunter or shepherd, but the useful articles his skill produced were eagerly demanded by those who could use with advantage instruments, for the making of which they had little skill or taste.

Thus before mankind was very old a very interesting economic condition had come into existence.

Moreover, as man progressed materially and intellectually he began to realise how unsatisfactory exchange in the form of barter is. How many arrow-heads should be given for a sheep skin ? If one man built a wattle hut for a man who owned cattle, but had no taste even for primitive building construction, how could the latter recompense the builder for providing the hut. Man felt the need of a standard of value and a medium of exchange long before he could have explained what he wanted. From experience of the methods utilised nowadays among the hunting fraternity in far-off countries it is obvious that in the hunting stage there was a rough-and-ready form of money found in the skins of animals. Some were rarer than others, and gradually a chain of values in furs would be agreed, and skins began to be used as currency. This method of using the obvious things of everyday life as media of exchange adapted itself to the succeeding stages— sheep and cattle, corn and fruits of various kinds were readily accepted and made use of as money. The final stage was reached when it dawned upon mankind that something outside ordinary consumable foods was necessary to provide a convenient form of money. By this time mankind discovered the utility of metals, and among these the precious metals gradually won their way as the most convenient articles to serve as the circulating medium. When mankind had arrived at this stage the economic situation was becoming increasingly full of interest. For nearly all the economic problems occupying attention now were emerging or had emerged. Some men were naturally thrifty, others thriftless. The latter began to realise that the former had advantages of which their improvidence had deprived them. How could they enjoy the results of thrift ? The fatal policy of borrowing began. Debtor and creditor experienced new sensations. A credit was found to confer power—a debt was apt to sap a man's independence. So dangerous did the position become that early lawgivers gave their attention to the problem. The usurer had begun to flourish, and his power to be realised. Indian, Semitic, and Greek sages pronounced their opinions in no veiled language on the proceedings of the forerunners of the modern money-lender. Aristotle declared that as money was a sterile substance the exaction of interest on money loans was unnatural. Moses, with far-seeing eye, declared that the exaction of interest from a brother Jew was wrong, but not from a Gentile. The economist by this time was, at any rate, semi-conscious—the stage of the unconscious economist was over—and hence-forward there was to be a growing desire to elucidate phenomena which were pressing themselves upon the attention of the world.

From another side the problems of life were becoming increasingly complicated. The family had developed into the tribe, the tribe into the race. In South-Eastern Europe the city state had made its appearance. The simple barter of earlier days had developed into trade and commerce. Slavery had been introduced into the social system, and many of the less pleasant occupations, especially those deemed unworthy of the attention of those enjoying citizen rank, were left to the slave element. As has already been hinted, politics began to evolve economic theories, and some of these were destined to affect mankind even to the present day. It was then that the contempt of the professional man for trade and business took its rise, a contempt which in its origin might have had a certain amount of justification, but for which under ordinary conditions there is no excuse.

The fourth stage dawned as gradually, perhaps more gradually, than its predecessors, and man entered upon a new epoch. Trade and commerce, industry and manufacture were to become the chief material interests of mankind.

When the renaissance awakened a sense of nationality, and the social divisions in Europe became vertical instead of horizontal, governments ambitious of extending their frontiers found themselves faced with the necessity to provide the sinews of war. To provide a taxable fund, industry and commerce promised better than agriculture, and so kings and nobles gave their attention to fostering new industries and to promoting trade both at home and abroad.

Then commenced to be laid the foundations of a policy which was destined to play a great part in the world's history for some centuries. The aim was to build up a strong self-contained, self-sufficient state, and the policy adopted in Western Europe is known as the Mercantile System or Policy of Power. So far as England is concerned the policy dates from the fourteenth century. Under Edward III new manufactures were introduced into this country.

Manufactured goods produced more wealth than the production of raw materials. The supply of goods and materials to the Continental markets, if carried on by English merchants and in English ships, was seen to afford the maximum of increase to the national wealth ; hence the Navigation Laws introduced during the reign of Richard II. Gradually the system concreted itself, and its greatest exponent was Cromwell. Navigation Laws, Corn Laws, Statutes of Apprentices, the Poor Law, and other similar legislation made up a definite policy whose object was the building up of a great and powerful England. A scaffolding was erected, thanks to which a fair building was achieved, and England became a great power on land and sea to be reckoned with by competitors for world-power, who were in their turn elaborating similar policies for the same purpose.

This country was the first to realise that a scaffolding is only erected to be dispensed with, and England's growth as a colonising and commercial power is to a great extent due to her readiness to discard or modify, before it becomes petrified, any policy which shows signs of having outgrown its original utility.

Towards the end of the seventeenth century two events set Englishmen speculating with renewed interest on economic subjects. In 1694 the Bank of England was founded, and in 1696 it was decided that a re-coinage was necessary. These two events produced discussions and led to the publication of economic views. Men like Sir William Petty had a few years previously been speculating and theorising about the national wealth ; Petty, indeed, made the utility of statistics known to his generation by the publication of his *Political Arithmetic*. The sanest of these writings had a leaning towards a newer and a freer policy ; thus free trade doctrines in an embryonic form made their appearance, and whilst meeting with scanty attention at home were carried across the channel and had a marked effect, which about the middle of the eighteenth century showed itself openly in the activities of *Les Economistes*, or as we call them, the Physiocrats. These men, in turn, had their effect on Adam Smith, who, when conducting the youthful Duke of Buccleuch on his grand continental tour, discussed economic subjects with the Physiocrat leaders in Paris. The results of Smith's thought and experience were embodied in the book which he published some ten years later—*The Wealth of Nations*.

II

ECONOMICS

EVERYONE becomes sooner or later conscious that he has needs, and these needs he finds can for the most part be satisfied if he can obtain certain things. When a man realises this he considers how he may supply himself with the things of which he feels the want. Experience soon teaches that the most satisfactory way to obtain what is required is to work for it. Thus needs lead to efforts, and successful effort brings a man satisfaction. Those things which a man strives after, so far as the material world is concerned, can be summed up in one word—wealth.

Political economy, or economics as it is now more popularly called, is concerned with wealth, its production, its distribution, and its consumption. In a community where wealth is produced under good conditions, with harmonious co-operation among those who are occupied in its manufacture, where the distribution of the wealth produced is carried out with equity and fairness to all concerned in its production, and where, lastly, the community consume what has been produced wisely and temperately, there you get a model community or State. This is a counsel of perfection probably never realised in this world, but it is an ideal for man to strive after. A great deal of the industrial unrest with which modern communities are so familiar is really in essence a healthy striving to attain to this ideal. That is one of the hopeful sides of modern developments ; indeed, the social and industrial history of the nineteenth century in the United Kingdom shows that though the progress may have been slow, some people perhaps think too slow, yet there has been a steady advance in the desired direction. A comparison of social conditions in the year 1800 with those of the year 1900 proves that there has been a gradual improvement in the distribution of wealth and a growing appreciation of those tendencies and laws the observance of which can do so much in the promotion of the higher side of human nature. The material, the intellectual, and the spiritual are much more closely allied than is usually recognised or taught.

Thus economics in ordinary everyday speech is the study of man from a business point of view. Be that man a statesman, a lawyer, a doctor, or a manufacturer, be he an artisan, a railwayman, a miner, or a sailor, what is his contribution to the wealth of the nation of whom he is a part, what does he enjoy as a result of his work, and how does he expend what he gains—in other words, what standard of comfort does he enjoy ?

The field appears wide enough and is complicated by that extraordinary phenomenon, human nature. Yet it should be possible to sketch a simple picture which, freed from complications and the difficult problems encountered in everyday life, may prove helpful to workaday men and women. One of the great needs to-day is clear and right thinking on economic subjects. Far too long has the charlatan, and the well-meaning but ignorant reformer, been allowed to hold the attention of men eagerly desirous of knowing economic truths.

The first necessity is to gain a clear understanding of what is meant by the word wealth. The man in the street has one very definite conception of wealth. To him it means abundance. Given a man who possesses a good motor-car, one or two fine houses, a good business, and a satisfactory banking account, there, says the ordinary individual, is wealth. Such a definition, however, is not sufficiently definite for the present purpose. It obviously does not include all wealth and it is confined to a generalisation concerning one man. Moreover, need abundance be an inseparable characteristic of wealth, and how is that abundance to be gauged ?

A well-known professor held that a knowledge of things was to be obtained by defining the word wealth, and he was right.

Another economist, John Stuart Mill, has given a good simple definition of the word which will suit us admirably to commence with.

" Wealth consists of all things useful and agreeable having exchange value." If this definition be accepted, the importance of abundance disappears. Wealth may be a very small as well as a very big thing. A single pin, ten of which, even under the profiteering conditions of war time, are given as the equivalent of one farthing change in a draper's shop, has exchange values, it is useful, and is therefore wealth. A single sheet of paper, now worth considerably more than in 1914, but still sufficiently cheap, has exchange value and is wealth. So is a motor-car or a fine yacht or an Atlantic liner. All these material things, if they possess exchange value, are wealth, and in the aggregate make up the wealth of the community. It is this wealth that we have to analyse : how is it brought into existence, to whom does it belong, what ought to be done with it ?

There are some economists who would include certain abstract qualities in the wealth of the individual or of the community, energies, skill, habits, and mental attain-ments. To do so, however, would add an unnecessary complication and need not be considered in an elementary textbook—it is sufficient for the beginner to know that some of the best economic thought does incline to include in wealth other than purely material things.

We restrict ourselves, then, to material and exchangeable things. But Mill's definition brought in a little word that requires some explanation. What is value ? For this is apparently inseparable from wealth. Thus at the outset of our work we should get, at

any rate, a preliminary idea as to what value
is. And here great care is necessary, for
value may be used in two very different
senses. Most things have both a use value
and an exchange value, and in order to prevent
misapprehension, it is now becoming the rule
to use the word utility for use-values, and
restrict value to exchange-values. It is
well, then, to bear in mind the special meaning
of these two words, utility and value. In
making exchanges, under modern conditions,
we employ money, one of the chief functions
of which is to serve as a circulating medium
or medium of exchange. Money values and
prices are of great importance, and in order
to realise that there may be a difference
between value and price, it should be pointed
out that for ordinary purposes it is well to
remember that whilst a value may be only
an estimate, price is a fact. For instance,
I purchase a motor-car for £500. The £500
is the money value of the car at the moment
of purchase and is a fact. If, after I have
driven the car a few weeks, I wish to sell it,
the original price may assist me in putting
a value on the car, but it will not necessarily
be the price I shall obtain. I probably value
my car at £450, but shall I obtain that sum
for it ? That will depend on a variety of

circumstances. What is the demand for and supply of cars ? What is its condition ? I value it at £450, but a man may offer me £400 cash for it, and if I accept the offer it becomes the price of the car and is a fact ; whereas my valuation of £450 was only an estimate.

Values, either utilities or in exchange, are most important, for in a manufacturing business man does not create matter. He changes the form or place of certain things and thereby creates values. The economists of the eighteenth century seem to have credited mankind with the ability to create, or at any rate to assist, in creating matter. Science has since proved that this is impossible. Man can accumulate wealth and he can add more value to existing forms of wealth. The recognition of this limitation has had considerable effects, notably in the conception of what is productive and what is unproductive labour.

Another volume will deal more fully with value ; here all that need be said is that value emerges or is increased when in connection with some commodity there is a combination of human need and human effort, or to put it another way, the cause of value and exchange is utility combined with limitation in quantity. It is most necessary that this fact should be clearly grasped at the outset of an enquiry into economics, for it was by ignoring this that a certain group of social reformers went astray. They asserted that value was caused entirely by man's efforts, implying that the cause and basis of value is labour. When from this it came to be assumed that labour meant manual labour only, there developed the misconception that as manual labour produces all wealth, all the wealth that is produced ought to belong to the labouring classes, and that all other members of the community are either exploiters of labour or are living on the wealth created by labour. As an illustration of this important point, an episode may be mentioned which occurred at a recent meeting where employers and representatives of Trade Unions were conferring. One of the labour representatives in the course of his speech, picked up a handsome cut-glass water bottle that happened to be on the table, and exclaimed : " Think what labour does when it produces such a beautiful and valuable thing." " Rather," said one of the employers present, " think of the value of the brain power and organising ability that first of all designs and then makes it possible for labour to carry out such work " : thereby illustrating the necessity for harmonious co-operation between all human agents necessary for the production of wealth.

III

THE PRODUCTION OF WEALTH

HAVING defined wealth, we can proceed to a consideration of how it is produced. Pins, paper, corn, and raw materials of all kinds have to be produced or provided. How can this be done in the best manner in each instance ?

There is one feature common to the production of all forms of wealth. Whether it be the making of pins, the construction of a ship, or the growing of corn, you must have a place to work in or upon, there must be labour, either your own or some one else's, and there must be tools and materials to work with. Hence it is at once realised that there are three things without which no production of wealth can take place. These three things the economist calls the factors of production, and they are :—

(i.) Land—the place to work in or upon.

(ii.) Labour—the human effort prepared to make ready the ground for agricultural purposes, and then sow and tend the crop till ready for harvesting, or in the case of manufactures the labour is required to carry out the operations necessary for changing the form of the raw materials in order to produce the finished article.

(iii.) There must be Capital—that is, accumulation of foodstuffs to feed the labour employed, the raw materials out of which the goods are to be made, and the tools and machinery, the factories and other kinds of premises and plant which must be available before the work of production can be undertaken.

The three necessary factors then are land, labour, and capital. Without all three, no results can be obtained. These three factors differ very much from each other. The first two are the most nearly akin when the aim is to produce foodstuffs or raw materials, because they both do something actively. Capital is a passive factor—by itself it does nothing : the hand of man is required to set it in motion.

Thus land and labour are said to be agents in production, because they do something— each contributing something which alone can do. Capital is said to be an instrument in production because it needs to be set to work by the hand of an active agent.

Thus there are three factors in production. Two of them are agents and one is an instrument. When these three factors are set to work and something is produced, a number of interesting phenomena emerge. Our task is to observe the working of the three factors, and to find out how they may be best set to work in order to bring forth the best results from every point of view.

Since experience teaches that this is a well-ordered world, there should be methods of procedure which will commend themselves to common sense.

These common sense ways for setting to work are really the laws natural to production. If we discover them and observe them we shall produce or manufacture in the most natural or, as is sometimes said, the most paying way. If through either ignorance or foolishness we disregard them, and attempt to work on a scheme of our own, ignoring the teachings of knowledge and experience, we shall inevitably suffer loss. We shall not at the best do as well as we might have done, and most probably our efforts will result in failure. The best and most satisfactory results can only be obtained by getting to know the natural laws of the industry we are practising and then set to work in conformity with those laws. In other words, we must make use of past experience, and only modify previous practice when we are quite sure that we have found a better way, more in conformity with natural law.

Economic laws or the best way to proceed in business can be ascertained. It has taken mankind a long time and has cost many a failure to discover them ; indeed, it is possible that even yet we are only on the threshold of our knowledge of them. The successful man of business or the prosperous farmer is the man who works in harmony with known laws, and is on the alert to detect and act upon new laws emerging under changing conditions.

When the factors of production have been set in motion and a body of wealth has been produced, we are faced with another set of phenomena. For the wealth then produced belongs to somebody, and who is that somebody ? This brings us to the problems connected with distribution. If three factors have combined, and as a result something has been produced, that wealth is due to the factors that have been engaged. Something is clearly due to each factor, and the problem is how shall the result of the effort made be so distributed among the factors that there may be a fair and equal share given to each. The share that goes to land is called rent, the part due to labour is called wages, but these are not always called wages. The artisan gets wages, but the man who organised may get profits, or a salary, or a commission on results ; any of these are the return for his organising skill and are the wages of the labour of organisation. Capital, although an instrument, has assisted the work, and the result is partly due to it. Thus it is entitled to a share, and this is known as interest.

Hence we have three factors, and if these are to work to the best advantage they must work in accordance with known or ascertainable laws. In addition to these laws we want to discover the best way to divide up the wealth which has been produced among those who have worked together in its production. Thus we are face to face with problems of the most fascinating interest ; problems affecting the welfare of every member of a healthy community. For the very continuance of the community, and the best material interests of its members depend on our wisdom and skill in getting at facts and then applying our knowledge in order that society may be based on a system of equity under which each member of the community may receive his rightful share of the wealth produced by the common effort.

Could any study be more interesting or more profitable ? And yet all too little is known by the average man of a subject which affects him at almost every point. A very large proportion of the evils from which we suffer, nay, most of the discontent and frictions which keep the modern world seething are due to ignorance of economic laws and tendencies. This state of affairs ought to be rectified. The fact that among working men there is a growing desire to study industrial history and economics is of good augury for the future. When every member of society makes it his business to know his rightful economic position, when he can apply his knowledge to know what is the due of other members, then he will be able not only to discuss questions of wages, profits, rents, and interest with knowledge and authority, but he will be in a position to decide as to what his own place shall be in the community. It may be asked, however, who is to decide as to the relative proportion in which the three factors of production shall be employed in any given business enterprise. This question leads to a consideration of what the economist calls the Law of Substitution. This law affects all enterprises connected with the production of wealth. The farmer, the colliery company, the manufacturers all practice the law either consciously or unconsciously. The successful man is the one who applies it with knowledge, if not perhaps that there is such an economic law, at least from experience of the effects of its working. Briefly stated it is to the effect that when land is plentiful or cheap, but labour and capital are scarce, wherever possible the factor, land, shall be utilised in large areas and labour and capital each or both shall be used more sparingly. Or, on the other hand, if labour be plentiful and capital scarce a greater proportion of labour shall be employed ; or should capital be plentiful and labour scarce, then labour-saving machinery shall be utilised to a greater extent. The following may be taken as a practical illustration of the working of the law in the case where land is cheap and building is costly. A manufacturer about to plan new premises under these conditions will take a bigger area of land and build simple one floor factories ; whereas if land be dear and building cheap he will be content with a small area of land and build a factory of several floors. When the factory is ready for installing plant and machinery, if labour be plentiful and wages low but capital is scarce and interest high, he will employ as much labour as possible but will reduce his expenditure on tools and machinery to a minimum. In farming operations the problem to be decided will be, shall I have a big area of land and be satisfied with a light crop or shall I take less land but by using greater quantities of manure and by employing more labour raise a heavier crop. Success in either case will depend on right judgment, or in applying the Law of Substitution rightly.

A very good practical illustration of the working of the law was given some years ago when the American steel masters visited Europe. During their tour on the Continent they inspected a big steel plant in Germany. One of the American steel masters was astonished at the number of workmen employed. He informed one of the German managers that he could reduce the cost of steel production very materially by introducing certain machinery. The German demurred and asked the American if he could produce figures to support his contention. Both parties went carefully into costs and the German was able to prove that owing to the low cost of German labour the American labour-saving machinery, so necessary in the States, would not be an economy if utilised under existing conditions in Germany.

It is the same law which influences the manufacturer as to the ratio in which various classes of labour shall be employed. For instance, if artisan labour be relatively cheap and the labour of superintendence relatively dear, there will be a minimum of foremen employed; if, however, ordinary labour be relatively dear, the number of foremen and supervisors will be increased. The object in view is to employ each of the factors to the best advantage. In arranging this there arise interesting points connected with each factor, but especially in connection with labour. This brings out a manager's organising and managing skill, for good organisation means that the organiser realises this part of his problem and is competent to deal with it. It is the organiser of industry who sets in operation the Law of Substitution, and the continued success of the business, once established, will depend on the foresight of the organiser in knowing when and where to modify the ratios in which the three factors are employed.

IV

LAND—A FACTOR IN PRODUCTION

ALL food and all the raw materials used in manufactures come from land or water. So far as food is concerned, land gives us meat, corn, and root crops, fruit and vegetables ; rivers, lakes, and sea furnish us with fish. From the land we mine coal, iron ore, and minerals generally. The farm, the mine, and the fishery give the great variety of products needed by mankind.

But all land is not equally fruitful either as furnishing crops or minerals. And, moreover, no sooner do we begin to study this natural agent in production which we summarise under the term *land*, than we become aware that not only are there lands of different degrees of fertility or productiveness, but there are certain eccentricities connected with any given area of land which become apparent as soon as we begin to cultivate it. Land that has hitherto been uncultivated is known as virgin soil. We begin to farm it, and we find that the productiveness is seemingly inexhaustible. Each season the crop may grow larger, and for a time there is an increasing return in reply to the work and manure we put into this special plot of ground. At first we are tempted to conclude that there is a law of increasing returns from land, and that all we have to do is to cultivate more and more intensively as the demand for the products of the land increases. After a time, however, we find that although we may not have reached the limit of productiveness on this special area of land, yet our efforts are repaid on progressively harder terms.

Two laws affecting land are gradually forced upon our attention. The first of these is known as the Law of Diminishing Returns, the second is the Law of Rent.

I. John Stuart Mill gave his attention to these phenomena and as a result enunciated the Law of Diminishing Returns from land. He found that up to a certain point the return on each extra unit of labour and capital put into the land was a more than proportionate increase, but after a certain time, although there might be a greater aggregate crop, yet there was a smaller return for each unit expended in cultivation. Mill, to illustrate the working of this law, made use of an india-rubber band. He pointed out that the rubber could be stretched almost indefinitely, at first with but little effort, but after a certain point had been reached each additional inch you stretched the rubber required an effort greater in proportion to that previously needed.

You can stretch or develop the productive qualities of land, but a point will be reached after which added doses of capital and labour will not earn a proportionally great return. This is called the point of diminishing returns. There may be a greater aggregate crop, but there will not be so much for each unit of effort employed as there was before the point of diminishing returns was reached. Thus, so far as agriculture is concerned, there is a limit beyond which it is not profitable to employ increased amounts of capital and labour on any given farm. There might result a greater crop, but there would be less for each cultivator when the result was distributed. To take a simple illustration free from complications, imagine fifty acres of land cultivated by five men, and for simplicity's sake restrict the illustration to land and men, leaving the use of capital on

3

one side. The theory is that after reaching a certain point in cultivation, the employment of extra labour may produce a heavier crop but there will be less for each man at harvest time. The five men working on the fifty acres produced one thousand bushels of corn—and the point of diminishing returns had just been reached. Another man comes along and joins the original five. Theory says that there may be a bigger crop but there will be less for each man when the result is divided. That is to say, the six men may manage to harvest eleven hundred bushels, a greater aggregate return, but when the crop is divided up between the cultivators, instead of receiving two hundred bushels each they will only receive a little over one hundred and eighty bushels, a bigger crop, but less for each man employed. If two more men come along the quantity of corn harvested may be increased to fourteen hundred bushels, but although the crop is so much greater there will only be one hundred and seventy-five bushels each when divided up. By continuing the experiment it would be found that on an area of land capable of supporting a few men in comfort, after the diminishing returns point had been reached, you might raise a considerably greater crop by employing a larger number of men but they would have to put up with a lower standard of living. In practical life this can be seen in parts of Western Europe where the land has been parcelled up into small areas. The land itself is very fertile and the crops produced intensively are extraordinarily great, but the cultivators are poor, in some cases living under conditions inferior to those of wage paid labourers.

An American economist attempted to dispute the truth of this theory. He had a certain amount of foundation for his contention because he was examining conditions in a new country where the action of the law was only just beginning to be felt in some agricultural areas. What he really did was to explain the history of land settlement in a new country, for he pointed out that settlers usually cultivate the fertile swampy soils last, as they avoid as long as possible the expense of clearing and draining. Had he investigated farming conditions in old countries where the law had for long been in operation, he would have told another tale. Moreover, Carey himself confirms Mill's theory when he admits that in a progressive community the price of the products of land tends to increase. This, of course, occurs when the cost of production, that is the amount of labour and capital required per unit of production, increases. If additional labour and capital resulted in a given area of land producing more in proportion than it did with a smaller expenditure, then there would be an increasing return, showing that the diminishing point had not been reached, and prices would tend to fall.

The practical effects of the law can be noted by studying the European corn market during this past half century. As greater demands were made on local grown food-stuffs prices went on increasing. But after the middle of last century, when owing to inventions which improved and cheapened methods of transport, Europe was able to import foodstuffs from lands where increasing returns were still the rule, prices in free European markets fell, and in a free trade market like that of the United Kingdom, food became abnormally cheap. As, however, population has grown in new countries and greater demands are being made for food, prices have practically ceased to decrease. Not only the cultivation of virgin soil, but the inventions of the chemist and the applications of science to farming may affect the question. It is conceivable that another

Carey may dispute the action of the law should scientific discoveries have further success. But, although new methods might postpone the return of the law, they could hardly do so indefinitely.

The effect of the law on agriculture and mining is easily observable. For with mining, when the minerals have to be sought at lower levels, the output in return for each unit of labour and capital becomes less. A good instance of this is the Lake ore ranges in America. At first the iron ore being on the surface the cost of mining was comparatively small. A cheaply constructed railway and mechanical shovels to fill trucks produced iron ore at a minimum of expense. When, however, the demand on the ore in these ranges grew to an immense annual quantity, the operation became less simple and the ore cost more to mine.

The law then, after the diminishing point has been reached, affects the cost of all foodstuffs and raw materials. The farmer and the miner are very directly affected.

The question may be asked, to what extent does the law affect the manufacturer ? The answer to this question is easy, yet difficult. In manufactures where it is possible to apply a progressive system of division of labour (see p. 105) there is a continuous increase of production. Given an expanding market with a steadily increasing demand it is possible to decrease the cost of production per unit. But the application of division of labour is limited by the extent of the market. Thus there comes a time when standardisation, admitting of repetition output, cannot be carried further; thus other things remaining constant increasing returns would cease. This, however, opens up a very large question in advanced applied economics which need not be dealt with here. The important thing to be noted now is that since the law affects the raw materials of manufacturing industries, it must affect the manufacturer, and the extent of this can be explained. For the purpose of illustration it is best to take some commodity which can be manufactured into a variety of forms. Some of these may be comparatively cheap, and others expensive. The effect of the law can then be examined. Iron supplies one of the best instances, for iron can be used in any form from crude iron, only one step away from the ore, up to watch-springs which have passed through many expensive processes of manufacture. A rise of ten per cent in the price of iron ore will very materially affect the cost of steel rails, but it would hardly be noticed by the makers of watch-springs or even of knife blades or of expensive steel instruments.

It has been calculated that five shillings' worth of iron manufactured into rails would be worth five and sixpence, but if the same quantity of iron was worked up into horse shoes it would be worth about twenty-three shillings, whilst if it were made into knife blades its value rose to be nearly one hundred and fifty pounds. In all these articles it is only the original five shillings' worth of iron that would be affected by the law; thus while a ten per cent rise in iron ore would affect the price of rails considerably, its effect on knife blades would be imperceptible. In other words, the further you get away from the crude raw materials in the processes of manufacture the less is the action of the law felt.

II. Rent is paid for the use of agricultural land, for the use of factories, and houses. There are thus two general problems to consider—country rents and town rents. In order that we may understand what is a rather complicated subject, we will consider the theory of agricultural rent first. And let us do so disregarding for the moment the payment of money to a landlord. Some people have a prejudice against landlords, and this might influence their judgment. It has been agreed that land is one of the factors necessary to production, and that land is no mere passive factor, but an active agent doing something in the work of production. Thus for the present purpose let us forget the landowner, and think of land as though it were a living thing doing something active in the work of production, and as such entitled to its share of what has been produced. For what has to be discovered is what share of the wealth produced is due to the natural agent—land.

It was David Ricardo who really made known the theory of rent. He did not invent it, but he gave it currency. He explained the method for measuring the pure economic rent of land, and he traced out the history of rent. Moreover, his theory has stood the test of time, nor can there be any doubt as to the truth of the law of economic rent as made clear by him. He did this by using hypotheses, by means of which he was able to imagine a simple condition of affairs and so got at simple facts. For the purpose of his argument he assumed that there is :—

(i.) Perfect competition in the letting of land.

(ii.) That all farmers are of equal capacity.

(iii.) That farmers supply their own capital.

(iv.) That the rent paid does not include any interest on capital sunk in improvements.

It is perhaps objected that these four assumptions seldom, if ever, occur in practical life. This may be so, and yet by making use of these assumptions it is possible to consider a simple problem, and if any tendencies or laws emerge, their practical existence can be tested by adding the complications inseparable from ordinary experience. If you commence with a complicated problem, progress may never be made, or you may produce a theory that the average man cannot follow.

To trace out how rent commenced, one must go back to the agricultural stage and picture an agricultural district where a number of people have settled and formed a village. These settlers till the surrounding fields and produce their own corn supply. When the village first came into existence, and the heads of families were looking round for land to cultivate, they naturally began to work on the best available land close to the village. There was probably plenty of this best quality land, and so all those cultivators requiring land obtained what they wanted and there was good land to spare. Under these circumstances no one paid rent; indeed, the phenomenon rent had not emerged. There was plenty of land for all, and all could get land of equal fertility. The little community, however, grew in number and a larger supply of corn was necessary; eventually all the best quality land near to the village was under cultivation. Up to that point rent did not emerge. However, when this point was reached the population of the village continued to grow, and the amount of corn required for food had also to be increased. As soon as all the best quality land was under cultivation several interesting problems would arise, even though the simple villagers remained unconscious of them. The cultivators of the land would have to plough up some second quality land to supply the demand, and the corn grown on this less fertile land would cost more to produce. The price of corn would go up in the local market, because there can only be one price for one commodity in one market at one time. Naturally the man who was growing corn on the newly cultivated but less fertile land could not sell it at a price based on the cost of growing corn on the better land.

All the corn would be sold at a price based on the cost of growing it on the less good land. Let us use modern money and measure in order to get a simple illustration. Suppose the corn had been selling at twenty shillings a quarter—that price being based on the cost of growing it on the best land, and now it was found that the corn grown on the less fertile land could not be sold at less than twenty-five shillings a quarter. The market price of all the corn would at once become twenty-five shillings. So that those farmers who were fortunate enough to be cultivating the better quality land would be better off than the other farmers to the extent of five shillings for each quarter of corn produced. That extra five shillings was not due in any way to the farmers' skill. It was solely due to the better quality of the land, and is the economic rent of that land. It is the share that the land is entitled to as an active agent in production.

It is possible to continue this story. The village grows into a town, the two qualities of land are no longer sufficient to produce the needed corn supply, thus land of still less fertility has to be laid under plough. Eventually the worst land cultivated for the market produces a corn that cannot be sold at less than forty shillings a quarter. By that time the economic rent of the best land has increased to about five times what it was, and the second quality land has become rent-bearing. The point that must be realised is that rent emerges as soon as lands of different degrees of fertility have to be cultivated to supply the same market. If the farmers own their farms this rent is not observed. It is realised that some farmers are more prosperous than others, and if the question were asked, how is it that there is this inequality as a result of farming, it would be answered that some cultivators had the advantage of farming better quality land. But the extra prosperity is not due to the human factor in production, i.e. the farmer, but is due entirely to the good quality of the land he is fortunate enough to have the right to farm. Should the farmer who holds this land retire, he can let his land at a rent based on the extra fertility it possesses plus an amount representing a return on the labour and capital he has put into the land, making it more eligible for farming. It is this last amount that complicates the subject of economic rent. If a man has cleared a forest, drained and hedged the land, put up necessary buildings and established a farm in good working order, no one would grudge him a fair return for the labour and expense incurred. There is, however, in the ordinary rent paid for a farm not only his return for work done by the human factor, but there is on land of superior quality an extra productiveness which gives an annual return not due to human labour.

Who ought to have the result of this extra fertility is not the question we are discussing here. What is for the moment necessary is that it should be clearly understood that there is this phenomenon in connection with land of superior quality and that someone will get the benefit of it. If the law was to disallow the payment of rent, what would happen would be that where a farm changed hands the new tenant would get the advantage of all improvements that had been added to the land, together with the pure economic rent. In other words, it is impossible to suppress the economic rent of land ; it is a natural phenomenon which emerges as soon as the demand for foodstuffs and raw materials renders it necessary to cultivate land of varying quality to supply a given market. As to who shall have the benefit of this natural phenomenon will depend on the law and custom of the community in question. This raises the question of " un-earned increment." For unearned increment attaches to both agricultural and town lands, though it is much more in evidence in the latter.

Before leaving the question of agricultural rent, let us consider an illustration from practical experience. There is a farm of say two hundred acres let at a rent of four hundred pounds a year. Can it be said that the economic rent of each acre is two pounds ? By no means. The farm consists of pasture, arable, and woodlands. And even among these three classes of land are areas of different values. If you begin to investigate into the annual value of the farm and are assisted by a man skilled in land value, many points illustrating the above argument come into notice. First of all there is the farmhouse and buildings, the hedges, the drainage and other improvements, which have been neces-sary for the establishment of a farm. An expert can assess the value, both capital and annual, of these buildings and improvements. Then, if you went over the farm acre by acre with the expert, he would point out that of the arable land some acres were worth more than others, and the same would be true of the pasture and woodlands. After a careful survey it would be possible to say what was the true economic rent of each acre. But while the crude average to the superficial observer who only took into account a farm of two hundred acres and a rent of four hundred pounds a year, would be two pounds for each acre, your careful investigation would give a much more interesting picture. It would differentiate between what was due to the land and what was due to man's thought and labour on that land. In other words, it would enable you to say what was the true economic rent of each acre, and what was due as a payment for capital sunk in the farm. Moreover, in the case of most farms another interesting fact would emerge. It would be pointed out by the expert that some of the land, although under cultivation, was not worth any rent. It only just paid to cultivate it. This land is said to be on the margin of cultivation, and it serves as a measure for the rent of all land of better quality. The land on the margin is cultivated because the demand of the market makes it necessary to do so, but it will not bear any rent. The cost of producing crops on that land is one of the factors, indeed, the main factor in fixing the market price of the crop produced. If demand for that special crop increases it may be necessary to cultivate land of still less fertility. When this is so, economic rent tends to rise. If, however, demand for those crops decreases, then marginal land falls out of cultivation and a land of better quality becomes the marginal land. In that case rents tend to fall. Remember, then, that cost of cultivating the land on the margin of cultivation is the factor which tends to fix market price, and that no economic rent is paid for the use of that land ; where a payment is made for the right to cultivate marginal land, it is interest on capital sunk and is not true economic rent at all.

Thus a definition of true economic rent is that it is the amount paid for the use of the productive powers of the land and consists of the difference between the cost of production on the land in question and the cost of production on the worst quality of land which is cultivated to supply the same market.

Always remember (i.) that corn is not dear because rent is paid, but that rent is paid because corn being in demand commands a high price ; (ii.) that no reduction would take place in the price of corn even though landlords were compelled to return all rent to farmers and it was decreed that for the future no farm rents should be exacted. What fixes the price of corn primarily is the cost of its production on the least fertile land whose cultivation is required by the demand of the market.

The cause of the payment of rent for cultivated land is simply that with the increase of population and the consequent increasing demand for foodstuffs and raw materials, inferior soils have eventually to be cultivated, and the price of the supplies needed by the community is primarily regulated by the cost of production of that portion of the supply which is produced at the greatest expense. It must be borne in mind that productiveness or quality includes both fertility and situation. Transport facilities have been greatly increased during the past half century, but distance from a market still affects the question, especially in times of stress. From this it is possible to arrive at the true economic rent of any plot of cultivated land. Indeed, from this survey of the subject it should be possible to work out both the history and the measure of rent.

The theory and practice of rent are on the whole in accord; it is, however, possible to point to instances where there is an apparent

4

contradiction or want of accord between economic theory and practical experience. This can in most instances be explained, for it is due to either sentiment or custom. As an instance of the former it is possible to point to parts of the United Kingdom where in some instances rents which are obviously excessive are paid, and the converse of this is also, but perhaps somewhat more rarely found. For it would be possible to point to farms where the rent paid is below the real letting value. In both cases it is usually found that sentiment is the root cause. Unduly high rents are exactable where people are deeply attached to their holdings, which may have been farmed by their forebears for several generations. In such cases an unscrupulous landowner can, and sometimes does, take advantage of an honourable sentiment, and exact an excessive rent. The law of rent is thus obscured, but whenever in such a case the sentiment which gave the landowner his opportunity ceases to operate, the law comes into play again. Nor is the law, as stated by Ricardo, really infringed, for he stipulated that there must be perfect competition in the letting of land (see p. 40). As to the converse, that is where the rent paid is less than the land is really worth, it is sentiment again that has intervened and obscured the working of the law. This is found where on old estates tenants have held farms for several generations and the land-owner influenced by sentiment does not exact the full letting value, being proud of the long connection between his family and those of his tenants. The explanation is the converse of that stated above, and whenever the letting of the farms comes into a free market the law asserts itself.

Custom, too, may obscure the law; for instance, in the case of metayer farming, where an agreed share of the produce is handed over to the landowner as rent. The metayer system so far as Europe is concerned is usually the mark of ineffective farming. It is an out-of-date system that has been replaced almost universally by tenant farming. But there is an interesting revival of the policy in a modernised form in the sheep and cattle areas in South America. The land-owner assigns to the metayer tenant a certain area of land together with a certain number of cattle or sheep for each acre. The tenant provides the necessary labour for carrying on the work, the tools, and a number of cattle or sheep equal to that provided by the landlord. Instead of paying an agreed rent,

there is an agreed proportion of the increase
of stock handed over to the landlord annually.

URBAN RENTS AND RATES

At first sight town rents seem to produce
a very different set of phenomena to those
just considered. It is true that *house rent*
includes interest on the capital sunk in building the house. There is, however, an element
in town rents—the pure economic rent—
which is due to causes closely allied to those
considered in connection with farm rents,
thus by careful analysis it will be seen that
the same law affects the tenancy of either
farm, house, or factory.

In an old country like England this is
perhaps not so easy to appreciate as in a
new country where towns have grown rapidly.
Our towns and cities have been for the most
part the growth of centuries, but in the new
world, towns have frequently developed into
great business centres in one or two generations, and thus cause and effect can be more
easily traced and explained.

Returning to the primitive village used
to illustrate the theory of agricultural rent,
it was seen that the early inhabitants who
were agriculturalists cultivated, in the first

instance, the most fertile land close to their cottages, and that as greater demands arose for foodstuffs, rent emerged. Suppose that as time goes on this village becomes a busy centre of population, and that industry and commerce have been added to agriculture and have eventually become the primary interests of the people, what are the intervening steps between the time when small rents were paid for the use of the site now occupied by the large town as farm land, and the present moment when, comparatively speaking, enormous rents are paid for the use of the few square yards required for houses or factories ?

The essential fact to notice is that the sparsely populated village has become a great centre of population. It is this that accounts mainly for the increased value of the land. With increasing population the agricultural village has become a great centre of exchange. The fertility of the land has not changed, but it has evolved a utility which possesses a much greater power in the production of wealth. " To labour expended in raising wheat or potatoes such land will yield no more of those things than at first, but to labour expended in the subdivided branches of production which require proximity to other producers, and especially to labour expended in that final part of production, which consists in distribution, it will yield much larger returns. The wheat grower may go further on, and find land on which his labour will produce as much wheat and nearly as much wealth ; but the artisan, the manufacturer, storekeeper, and professional man find that their labour expended here, at the centre of exchanges, will yield them much more than if expended even at a little distance from it; and this excess of productiveness for such purposes the landlord can claim, just as he could an excess in its wheat producing power. And so our settler is able to sell in building lots a few of his acres for prices which it would not bring for wheat growing if its fertility had been multiplied many times."[1]

Thus, when the village has grown into a Chicago, the original settler, or his descendant, has become a very wealthy man not from anything he has done except in originally making a happy selection of a site which has become a busy commercial centre. The increase and concentration of population is the explanation of what has occurred. The most valuable lands in the world, such as those

[1] Cf. Henry George, *Progress and Poverty*, p. 169.

of central London, Paris, and New York, yielding the highest rents, are not necessarily lands of surpassing fertility, but lands to which a surpassing utility has accrued owing to the increase of population. Another phenomenon quickly strikes the investigator into these problems. Even in cities there are great differences in the values and rents of land, for some sites have a greater utility for a given purpose than others. Shops, offices, and business premises in London, near to a busy railway terminus, where crowds of people are constantly passing are conveniently situated for attracting business. "To succeed, a shop must be in a main thoroughfare" is a commonplace statement. The extra business thus gained is not primarily due to the cleverness or ability of the tenant of the shop. He might be an exceptionally able business man, but his best efforts would be crippled were his shop in a side street. He needs a good situation for his shop; with that and with business ability success is assured. It is this extra value, due to position, that the landlord exacts. The fertile land has evolved a new quality. It has a utility of position which gives it a monopoly value. The high profits made in shops enjoying the advantage of good position are to a great extent due to that position, and it pays the tenant to agree to a high rent rather than take a bigger shop in a less eligible part of the town.

The truth of this can readily be grasped by watching the number of people entering shops such as confectioners and drapers in various parts of the same town, or even of the same street. It will at once be seen that the shop most convenient for shopping, that is the shop at the point where people are constantly passing in great numbers, is the shop best calculated to succeed. Thus, so far as economic rent is concerned, it must be realised that as a community progresses, there emerges in the case of land enjoying certain advantages of either fertility or situation, or it may be of both, an extra gain or profitableness in connection with production. This extra gain is not due to either the skill of the cultivator or the shopkeeper or manufacturer ; nor is it due to any genius attaching to the landowner. In some cases this extra profitableness goes on increasing even to a fabulous extent. It is due to progress and the growing density of population. It has been called an unearned increment. To whom ought it to go ? Where the land is privately owned it goes mainly to the owner. Where the land is the property of the State, municipality, hospital, or university, the community benefits. To exact all unearned increments for the community might prove to be a double-edged weapon, as there are losses to face as well as gains to pocket. It may be that an equitable arrangement will be found in a judicious system of taxation. The death duties seem to point in that direction. This method of procuring for the community, at any rate a share of this increment, is only in its infancy. It deserves study and careful development.

At the present moment it is very necessary that what economic rent is should be very clearly known. It cannot be abolished. Even though landlords were forbidden to exact rent it would still exist. It is due to progress and the general development of the community and not to man's labour or skill. Economic rent is inherent in the land, it increases or diminishes automatically. Like the sunrise it is a natural phenomenon quite outside man's jurisdiction, and it operates independent of any restrictions he may attempt to impose.

LOCAL RATES

In connection with conditions affecting town property, it should be made clear that rates ought to be looked upon as a deduction from the pure economic rent. In practice it is found that in some instances the landlord nominally pays the rates, whilst in others it is the tenant. Broadly speaking, the rule is that for small properties where the rent is paid weekly the landlord pays the rates, but that in the case of larger houses where the rent is paid quarterly the tenant has also to pay the rate collector. In both cases the payment really comes from the same source, and this can be seen by considering the circumstances of both classes of property. Really rates are a part of rent ; they are the share of rent exacted by the local authority for local expenditure. If a man takes a house at a rent of £100 a year he will find that it is assessed for rating purposes at about £80, and if the local rates stand at ten shillings in the pound he will have to pay £40 to the rate collector. A wise man, before definitely taking a house, enquires as to the assessment, and the amount of the rates, and if he finds that the two amounts come to more than he can afford for the use of the house he will look out for another house which is obtainable at a lower rent. He may attempt to bargain with the landlord, and if the landlord finds that he cannot obtain a tenant at £100 a year he will probably be willing to compromise, but if the house be let at £100 and the rates amount to £40 the tenant will have to find the sum of £140 per annum. After he has been in the house a few years, should the municipality undertake some improvements which entail a large expenditure of money and result in a serious increase in the rates, which have to be raised to fifteen shillings in the pound, there will be a demand for another £20 a year. During the continuance of the tenancy agreement the tenant will be bound to pay this sum, but when he has an opportunity of reconsidering his tenancy he will endeavour to shift part of it on to the landlord, especially if he cannot afford £160 a year to live in that house. What will the landlord do ? He will endeavour to find another tenant, and if he is successful he will let the original tenant go. But if the full competitive value of the house was £140 for rent and rates, which means that he cannot find another tenant, he will compromise in order to retain the original tenant. On the contrary, if rates were to decrease in amount, and, to take an extreme case, if on property belonging to the Corporation some valuable mineral was discovered in quantities sufficient to pay the whole of the local expenditure, then rates would go to zero. So long as the agreement between the landlord and tenant lasts the tenant would get the advantage of this, but the moment there was an opportunity to reconsider the agreement, provided that other things remained constant, that is to say it was worth the tenant's while to pay £140 to live in that house or that was the annual value of the house at competition, the landlord would be able to exact £140 a year from the tenant.

Where the landlord of weekly property nominally pays the rates the same thing is true. In the case of a street where the houses were let at seven shillings and sixpence per week each, that being the full competitive letting value of the property, and the rates were to increase five shillings in the pound, the landlord would not necessarily be able to raise the rents, other things remaining constant. The value of the houses was seven shillings and sixpence a week, and the landlord would not be able to exact more. If, owing to some town-planning scheme or extra facilities in the shape of tramways which enabled people to live further from their work, half of the houses of this street became empty, the landlord would be seeking tenants and the tendency would be for the rents to fall, but rates are for the most part fixed charges, and the amount of rates demanded of the landlord would remain practically the same, or would tend to rise. Falling rents and rising rates would be the result ; or, in the event of rates disappearing, as imagined in the other illustration, the seven shillings and sixpence a week rent would not necessarily be modified, because it was worth the while of the people to live in these houses at seven shillings and sixpence per week ; in other words, that was the full competitive value, and so long as other conditions remained constant the lessening or remission of rates would not result in the lessening of rents. In a case where rising rates impelled a landlord to try to raise rents his success would merely show that he had not previously been exacting the full economic rent.

The point to note is that the pure economic rent of a house, whether large or small, that is to say its full letting value at competition, includes both rent and rates. Thus the amount paid to the local authority for local expenditure is really a deduction from the purely economic rent.

V

LABOUR—A FACTOR IN PRODUCTION

LABOUR has been defined as a conscious moral act performed by man as a result of his ability to reason out the problems of life. Mankind is faced with material conditions demanding the active exercise of intelligence if there is to be progress and improvement in the conditions of living. All life, indeed, is endowed with the ability to do something, whilst intelligence and reasoning powers differentiate human life from all other kinds of life. Vegetation has life but it acts unconsciously; the lower animals enjoy the gift of life in a much higher form, but so far as we know have not made a great amount of progress from the time of the primitive type except where aided by man. The work of the lower animal in a state of nature is regulated not by intelligence but by instinct. The wild animal instinctively hunts for food, but his hunting is carried on in the same way now as it was a thousand years ago. Man alone in the animal world is endowed with the intelligence which enables him to take thought and give attention to making progress. He alone has studied the forces of nature and made them his servants. Man's labour then stands on a different footing from all other kinds of labour.

It is sometimes said that all the wealth produced is due to labour. This is, however, a saying that requires a good deal of amplification, for we must carefully define the word labour and understand exactly what is included in the term. There are people who accept the saying without apparently troubling to determine exactly what it includes. Indeed, they are apt to make use of this line of thought while taking it for granted that labour means manual labour and nothing else.

It may be taken for granted that land, which we have already seen is an active agent in the production of wealth, can only produce to advantage when assisted by man. As this assistance involves man's labour, an analysis of that labour will give a very good illustration of what is included in the general term labour.

As soon as mankind began to cultivate

land there was a response to his efforts. But primitive methods of agriculture were not very productive.

In order to get the best crops out of land many varieties of labour must be put forth by man. The chemist analyses the soil and tells the cultivator what the soil needs in the way of manures to give the best results. The inventor is required to devise the best tools and machinery for treating land and crops. Modern farming practice makes demands on the scientist, the inventor, the engineer, and a number of other people, as well as on the farmer and the labourers who do the actual cultivation of the soil. A great part of this work is done in the study, the laboratory, and the workshop. Hand and brain co-operate, and their full and harmonious co-operation is necessary if the best results are to be obtained. Manual labour, like land, as a factor in production, requires the assistance and co-operation of brain power and organising ability or its efforts will be severely handicapped and the results of the labour expended will be unsatisfactory.

The Physiocrats spent considerable effort in defining productive and unproductive labour. Succeeding generations of economists continued and developed the enquiry, until at

the present day a very interesting pronounce-
ment on the subject is to be found in most
manuals of political economy. What is now
classed as productive labour by competent
economic thought gives the best definition of
the labour force of a given community. As
a corrective of incorrect teaching, this part
of the subject should be carefully studied.
Nor should the student proceed further with
his work until he has grasped what the labour
force of a country really comprises.

The Physiocrats held very definitely that
only that labour could be classed as productive which was actually employed in the
production of foodstuffs and raw materials.
The labour connected with farm, mine, and
fishery produced solid returns, but the labour
employed in a factory, it was asserted, merely
changed the form of the raw material, it produced nothing ; nor did the labour of the
carrier or the sailor, for by transport labour
goods were simply taken from one place to
another—they remained the same goods, there
was no outward change. Manufacturing
labour it was conceded might be necessary,
but it was in a different class from that of the
cultivator of the soil or the miner.

And when the efforts of doctors, lawyers,
teachers, shop-keepers, and commercial people

5

came to be considered they were unceremoniously included in the unproductive class. The early English economists reconsidered the subject and had little difficulty in adding the work of those engaged in manufacturing industries to this class of productive labour. But even then there were two great groups of labour, one labelled productive and the other unproductive. To people holding these views it was not a little disconcerting when the scientist pointed out that mankind produces nothing, that matter cannot be increased, that the crop of corn merely represents elements taken from the soil, the air, and the rain : there is merely a change of form, comparable with that which changes the ores of various metals into a locomotive engine.

It was also pointed out that the miner only displaces coal or ore. He does not make it. His labour only differs in degree from that of the transport worker who transports the coal from the colliery to the domestic hearth or to the factory. And yet the miner had always been included in the class of productive labourers. Thus gradually the group of recognised productive workers was enlarged and made to include industrial and transport workers.

But what has to be said of commerce—the wholesale and retail trader, and the professional man ?   So far as the traders were concerned, it became obvious that some machinery was necessary to form a link between the producer and the consumer.   The textile mill produced cloth of various kinds in wholesale quantities.   The consumer required a few yards for some purpose, but the manufacturer had no system of organisation to supply the needs of the consumer.   Something was necessary to complete the cycle of production.   Hence the need for the wholesale and retail markets ; the warehouseman and the retail shop.   If a woman wants a small quantity of silk to make a blouse she does not want a whole roll of silk as supplied by the mill, and so she goes to the draper, who cuts off from the roll the exact quantity required.   If I want a cup of tea, it is no good to be told that a ton of tea is in the warehouse and can be had at such a price.   What I want is the possibility of obtaining a small quantity from which I can get a cup of tea without causing waste to the world's supply of tea. This I am able to get from the grocer, who thus completes the cycle of production and is a very useful and necessary member of society, whether he be the proprietor of one shop, or the manager of a multiple shop company, or of a co-operative store. Some machinery is necessary for supplying retail quantities of the ordinary goods of everyday life, and the shop or store provides just what is necessary. The labour connected with these establishments is therefore necessary and must be classed as productive. The corn output of America and Canada is only useful to Europe if transported thither ; the great quantities of corn and flour in our elevators and mills are only useful when handled by baker and grocer. These retailers are necessary workers, and are therefore now included in the productive class. Conditions may change, it may become necessary to modify the system of retailing the necessaries of life, but it is difficult to imagine a system under which retailing will be unnecessary, and so long as it be necessary, the labour connected with it can only be classed as productive.

Then we come to other types of workers—the teacher, the doctor, the minister of religion, the actor and musician, the magistrate, judge, and policeman, member of Parliament, State officials from the lowest to the chief of the State. What shall be said of all these ? The teacher in school and university influences the material out of which various types of future workers are being moulded. Few professions probably give rise to so much disappointment, but looking over a period of years, it is evident that education has achieved remarkable things for the community. The work of production has been very considerably assisted by the teaching of the school and classroom, and by the investigations carried on in the laboratory. The doctor and the surgeon have kept the community in better health and condition for work and effort than would have been the case had there been no one charged with this responsibility. The minister of religion has preached an ideal— he has inculcated morality and high thinking. In proportion as his efforts have led men to work more honestly and to take a saner view of life and its responsibilities he has had an effect on production. Modern society, too, requires the institutions connected with the maintenance of law and order. Without security the work of production could not proceed, hence the necessity for police, magistrates, and judges, Parliament and the government departments with their staffs of men skilled in administration. Were the efficiency of government adversely affected, production would suffer. A well ordered state is a necessity. Anarchism and material well-being could not exist together.

The actor and the musician too may have their sphere in helping on the productive work of the world. The worker with hand and brain gets wearied and needs recreation. To the extent that healthy amusement helps to recreate the jaded worker, the providers of that amusement are assisting in the productive work of the community.

Thus the modern teaching on this subject is that all those workers who either *directly or indirectly* assist the work of production should be classed as productive workers.

Can an unproductive worker be mentioned ? Yes, unfortunately there are those whose efforts tend to diminish the productivity of the community. The book, the picture, or the play that panders to the lower instincts, and thereby weakens the will and character of reader or auditor may result in weakening the ability of the worker. The agitator whose work is destructive, but who cannot suggest what can beneficially take the place of what he is trying to destroy. Such work as these is unproductive because it neither directly nor indirectly helps on the well-being and productiveness of the community.

Thus under modern conditions instead of spending time in discussing what labour shall be classed as either productive or unproductive, it is more essential to differentiate between the degrees of productiveness of available labour in order to prevent a waste of labour which would result if an undue proportion of available labour was employed in any one group. For instance, at the present moment, after five years of war, the world demands large quantities of foodstuffs and manufactured goods, but there must be a sufficient labour force employed in the distributing industries to circulate what is produced. In neither class should there be such an excess of labour that either there is an amount of wealth produced that cannot be transported to consuming centres, or there are not sufficient goods to be transported to keep transport labour fully employed.

As to the degrees of importance of various types of work, it may be suggested that the highest class of productive labour is that of the efficient organiser of production. The intelligence required to organise and carry on successfully a great business—either a manufacturing business or a great transport undertaking is of enormous value to the modern community, and must be placed in the highest class. There are many more failures than successes in this class of work. The efficient organiser is comparatively rare. He is not the monopoly of any one section of society. The most successful organisers have come from various ranks, many have been self-made men, especially in the United Kingdom. There have been no water-tight compartments in this country, binding men to remain in the position into which they were born. Here, as in no other country, brains and capacity like murder will " out." But the possessors of the qualities necessary to give business success of the highest degree are comparatively few in number. Theirs may not be a very high type of brain power ; that is an arguable point, but it is the rarest type.[1] Its value to the community is difficult to assess, the fact that men endowed with these qualities can command their own price, without any adventitious aid, emphasises their importance. Next comes the work of invention and discovery. Then the labour that is capable of carrying into effect the schemes of the first class and of utilising the inventions and discoveries of the second class. In this is included the skilled artisan of all trades.

[1] Cf. p. 131 f. the qualities required by the organiser of industry.

After these comes the class of labour employed in transport and commerce, the *necessary* official and professional classes, then those whose work recreates and keeps fit the active producers. In a well organised society there should be a minimum of difficulty in deciding as to which labour group a man's special talents warrant him attaching himself. Where mistakes are made it is evident that the community in question has not attained to the higher development, and there is need presumably of modification and improvement in the system of education.

The Share of Production Due to Labour

Theoretically the amount of what is produced that can be claimed by the labour force we have just considered, is the whole body of wealth produced after the shares due to land and capital have been deducted. The amount due to land depends on the fertility or utility of the land;[1] that due to capital is the market rate of interest[2] together with an addition proportionate to the risk involved in the industry in which it is em-

---

[1] Cf. Chap. iv.   [2] p. 140.

ployed. In some cases the risk may be small, in others it may be considerable. This insurance against risk requires careful consideration. For instance, the risk increases when producers do not co-operate harmoniously, and production is thereby hampered.

This view of labour, including all those engaged in the work of production from the organiser to the humblest labourer, might not at one time have been considered admissible. In the days of smaller businesses there was the capitalist employer, the man who carried on his own comparatively small business with his own capital, and whose share of the wealth produced was called his profits. That, however, has become, or is rapidly becoming, a thing of the past. The company or corporation now carries on most of the world's work. The capital is supplied by shareholders and the organisers are paid officials, subject nominally to the shareholders. This has wrought a great change in industrial conditions, but the change is a healthy one and should be completely satisfactory when it has been fully carried through. At present, industry is passing through a stage of transition; as to whether the ultimate outcome will be beneficial to all interests depends on how those interests face this period. If a sane and well informed policy be adopted, the issue may be thoroughly satisfactory to every grade of the labour involved. A mistaken idea as to the issues at stake, or as to the relative importance of the factors, may have the effect of arresting or restricting industrial development. This would adversely affect all sections of labour. What is required is healthy evolution along lines discernible to those who have knowledge of history and the working of economic laws.

The question of profits[1] will be dealt with later on. At this point the problem to be considered is that connected with wages.

The man who is paid daily or weekly for work remunerated by the hour or the piece is said to be a wage earner. The man who is engaged for an annual amount paid monthly or quarterly is said to be paid a salary. Hitherto the salary earner has made his own bargain for his services, and presumably has been paid what was considered to be his worth. Both theory and practice as to the conditions affecting the wage earner are full of interest, for new forces have come into play and the results have been momentous.

[1] Cf. Chap. vi.

The invention of the steam engine made possible the industrial revolution which accentuated as time went on the problems connected with manual labour and its share of production. But the wages question and its problems was no new thing even one hundred and fifty years ago, when Watt was successfully experimenting with steam. In France, men like Turgot were speculating on the causes of misery among the labouring classes, and they came to some conclusions that affected economic thought for many a decade : indeed, their views, developed by Adam Smith and Ricardo, were utilised by men of a very different stamp and for a very different purpose.

France in the middle of the 18th century was suffering from the exhaustion following a long period of conflict. The national debt had mounted to unheard-of figures, and the taxation was so heavy that the sole limit to the amount levied on the peasantry was their ability to pay. Labourers lived on the borders of starvation. What was the cause of this unhappy state of affairs ? Economic speculators observed current facts and tendencies ; they did not apparently give attention to the possibility that the country was passing through a stage of transition.

They agreed as though what was, always had been, and always would be. And so they concluded that the labouring population merely gain a bare subsistence. " In every industry it must happen that the wages of the worker are limited to the amount necessary for subsistence—Il ne gagne que sa vie." Here we get the foundations of a theory which earned for Political Economy the title of the Dismal Science—and no wonder. It is true theoretically, and probably in practical life too, that in the first instance labour secured the whole fruits of its effort. A man made his own simple tools or weapons, and what he produced with them was his own property. There were no deductions. But as society progressed things changed. Rent emerged, and had to be paid on certain qualities of land. Then industry and trade assumed greater proportions, and capital was needed to provide improved tools, machinery, buildings, stores of raw materials, vehicles for distribution, and other necessary adjuncts to a trading community. At this point, the advanced socialist may say, here began the exploitation of the worker. But a short consideration of facts will convince one that quite the contrary was occurring. The rent that was paid was no deduction either from the earnings of the farmer or from the wages he paid any labour he might have to employ. It was paid for the use of fertile land, and was due to the extra fertility of land for the payment of which the farmer and his labourers got the benefit in having to put forth less effort to produce crops. The same thing occurred when, owing to thrift, capital was available to assist manual and organising labour in manufacturing employments. Machinery, buildings, and supplies of raw material lightened the toil of labour and made it more regular and more productive. This meant the possibility of shorter hours and better pay. The interest paid to the thrifty man who saved capital was no deduction from the worker or his employer. Capital gave a double benefit—it blessed both lender and borrower where it was rightfully employed. The mistakes as to the exploitation of labour by capital arose out of the theory that capital not only provided machinery, buildings, and raw materials, but paid labour. That by so doing it was able to grind the face of labour. English economists took up the French theories and came to the conclusion that the labourer's share of the wealth he helped to produce was fixed by the capital available for his employment, and that if you divided the amount of this capital by the number of workers you knew the average wage. And this average would remain at a point at which it was sufficient to maintain the labouring classes, who would only gain a bare living. Ricardo introduced a new idea to the theory. He held that a class forms a notion of a *standard of living*, and that this standard regulates the increase of population. From these conceptions developed the Wages Fund Theory or Iron Law of Wages. There were three stages in the development of this theory.

Malthus[1] declared that " it may at first appear strange . . . that I cannot by means of money raise the condition of a poor man . . . without proportionately depriving others in the same class. But if I only give him money, supposing the produce of the country to remain the same, I give him a title to a larger share of the produce than formerly, which shows that he cannot receive without diminishing the share of others."

What Malthus assumed for the purpose of his argument was that the food supply is fixed in amount, so that an increase in the

---

[1] *Essays on Population*, iii. 5.

demand would raise price without increasing
supply ; and that a certain amount ot the
total supply is earmarked for manual labour.
Under modern conditions at any rate, those
assumptions do not hold good.

The elder Mill examined the theory and
confirmed it. But he made use of the word
capital instead of food supply. According
to him it is the amount of capital, i.e. the
wealth available for the work of production
which fixes the amount of wealth divisible
among the workers.

John Stuart Mill[1] laid it down that industry
is limited by capital, but does not always
come up to that limit, while the increase of
capital gives increased employment to labour.
He added that it is not all capital which
constitutes the wages fund of a country,
but only that part which is earmarked for the
direct purchase of labour. Thus wages
depend on the supply and demand of labour,
or on the proportion between population and
capital. Moreover, wages cannot rise but by
an increase of the aggregate funds employed
in paying labour, or in a diminution in the
number of men desiring to be employed.

Such a theory was admirably adapted as

[1] *Political Economy*, Bk. i, Chap. v., 1–3.

the text from which to preach class warfare, and it became, in fact, the foundation of the teaching of that school of social reformers, the fruition of which is having such disastrous effects at the present moment.

It is true that Mill confessed that he had gone too far, but others reiterated and amplified his conclusions and his repudiation has been to a great extent ignored—especially by interested parties.   Mill's recantation did not give even the germ of the truth, for he still maintained that wages are paid out of an existing fund which cannot exceed the means of the employing class.

Fortunately, new light was to be thrown on the subject, and it came from the other side of the Atlantic.   In 1876, F. A. Walker published a book on wages, showing that there is no necessary relation between capital and wages.   Wages are paid out of what is produced, not out of any pre-existing fund. For convenience sake wages may be advanced out of existing wealth, but only because the owners of that wealth know that the workers are engaged on productive employment, and that the advance will be repaid.   He holds that the workers are in effect the owners of the whole of the product subject to the payment of definite amounts due to land for

6

rent, capital for interest, and the employer for profits. Since Walker wrote commercial and industrial organisation and methods have progressed considerably. Half a century ago profits might be anything and were indefinite in amount. To-day, however, the situation is greatly changed. In place of the capitalist employer there is the limited company or the corporation. The accounts of these must be published, and the possibility of hiding earnings under a system of book-keeping or as secret reserves has been restricted and is likely to be still further restricted. The facts can be known if interested parties make up their minds to know them. The whole labour force of a community is in a position to get most of the required information, and can, if it so decide, obtain all relevant information. Unfortunately, instead of labour insisting on obtaining facts to which it is entitled and on which it could base a sound economic claim, it has hitherto been content to believe that capital exploits labour. It has suspicions, but very little concrete knowledge. It is those suspicions that are at the root of labour unrest and industrial friction. It is in the interest of the whole community, and especially of the whole labour force, that specious statements should be replaced by economic facts. This should be the aim of all well wishers of industry and commerce. From facts which could be ascertained, the economic rights of each member of the industrial force could be demonstrated, and in place of wild statements as to the exploitation of labour there might be substituted a demand based on sound economic knowledge. Limiting production, either by a ca' canny policy or by refusing to take advantage of the best processes and the most modern machinery, must result in decreasing the real wages of labour.[1] The greater the production of all necessary and useful commodities, the better can be the position and the higher the standard of living of every member of the community. And with increasing production there goes hand in hand an increasing cycle of prosperity; for the greater the production the less is the cost of producing, and so prices can fall. Increased wages with decreased production results in a more than proportionate increase in price. We may now[2] be suffering to some extent from profiteering. But the possibility of profiteering is limited. We are suffering because during five strenuous years we have

[1] Cf. p. 90.   [2] 1920.

been forced to concentrate our efforts on unproductive production, and we have been consuming unproductively. The cost of the war is the sum of our unproductive consumption. The victory of the Allies has saved the liberties of the world, but the effort put forth to crush autocracy and militarism has been costly and must be paid for. The war has, however, given a spur to invention, it has caused us to scrap uneconomic methods of working, and to equip our factories with the most productive machinery, and to make use of the most productive processes. Peace has dawned, and it behoves the world now to apply to the arts of peace, the machinery and processes found to be so necessary during the strenuous time of war. If any one country refuses to utilise these new methods it must suffer, for other countries will not be so foolish. In the United Kingdom we are in a new position of advantage. That unscrupulous men may attempt to grasp as much as possible of the resulting wealth for self is doubtless true, but whereas at one time this might be done with impunity, because of the difficulty of analysing the economic position, we now have the necessary information available, or the means for making it available. Hence, if the country will face peace problems as it faced war conditions, with a united front and a determination to grasp the facts and reconstruct in the light of those facts, there will be no need for class warfare or of the universal strike.

Those who believe that they are entitled to a greater share of the wealth produced should either by themselves or through their leaders make plain their economic position, and if their conclusions are sound they will obtain redress. But to imagine that with a modicum of knowledge, and that perhaps poisoned at the source, they can hold the community to ransom, is not only a mistake but a crime. It cannot succeed, and its failure will entail untold misery on the masses of the nation.

It may be objected that it is only possible in theory to get the full facts necessary for determining the economic rights of each of the factors in production. There is, however, a concrete illustration of what can be done. The government of the United States investigated the pottery industry[1] both in America and Europe. The result of this investigation has been published in full. From the voluminous report, not only can a

[1] *The Pottery Industry*, published by the Department of Commerce, Washington, Miscellaneous Series, No. 21, 1915.

great deal be learned as to the industrial and commercial working of an important industry, but employers have already realised that it is to their advantage to supply further information, and in this country the successful working of the Standing Joint Committee in the pottery industry is a monument of what can be achieved in this way. It is to be hoped that investigations and reports, carried through on the same lines, may be undertaken and published in connection with all our main industries. Nothing could be more helpful at the present moment, nor could anything be calculated to serve our industrial life better in the future.

The theory as to wages has developed from a hopeless stage which was the result of considering a passing phase as a permanent condition. This gave rise to the Iron Law of Wages, an initial attempt to account for a new series of industrial phenomena. The theorists did not make use of historical experience: they argued from the particular to the general, and gave circulation to a doctrine that could only lead to mischief. The one great service rendered was that it arrested attention and compelled investigation. It took over half a century to get at the truth, and meantime the error of the original theory had laid the foundations of a movement that was to strain the industrial world to breaking point. The workers in their efforts to save themselves from a situation that went far to confirm the theory, began to organise themselves into unions. This policy has had great success in improving conditions arising out of the revolution caused by the application of steam and labour-saving machinery to manufactures. Now after long years of experience Trade Unionism is on its trial. Its future depends on how it grapples with the present reconstruction period. Side by side with labour's own endeavour to improve working conditions has progressed the efforts of Parliament to make working conditions better by means of Factory Acts and industrial legislation. Middle-class sympathisers, feeling that labour might not be able to help itself, advocated a policy of association from which has resulted the Co-operative movement and modern Socialism. Both these have developed on lines very different from those expected by their founders.

The industrial history of the nineteenth century gives a series of attempts at practical amelioration, nor has this been without success. A very great advance has been accomplished as can be realised by comparing the position of manual labour a century ago with that of to-day. The marked improvement is due to all these forces, sometimes co-operating, oftentimes apparently working almost in opposition. The present situation is hopeful to the extent that causes have been marked and effects studied. A century ago the individual workman might be a victim to a rich employer. To-day organised labour knows and shows its strength. If that strength can realise the strength of other factors in industry and use its power with knowledge and moderation healthy evolution will result. The time is ripe for a great advance, but the possible outcome is endangered by the extent to which self-seeking on the one hand and an ignorant application of force on the other may bring about disastrous revolution instead of natural evolution. It is the economist's duty to point to economic laws and suggest an advance in accordance with them.

Individual bargaining, with the individual at a disadvantage, has been replaced by collective bargaining, but that policy is only in its infancy. Should the next step be towards what is known as syndicalism, i.e. each industry working for self against the community, and this is an anti-social movement, the future will see an intensification of the friction which has been working up for the past two decades. If the next step be towards State Socialism there will result a change in the direction of industries, followed by a species of enslavement weighing heavily on the whole community. *Industrial freedom* is the desired goal, and that can best be obtained by all the factors and all industries co-operating for the common good, with the State acting as the guardian of the consumer and the national well-being. Amidst the clang of faction this last seems destined to prevail.

In America the practical development of industries has differed from that in this country. The conditions were widely different. There was a new country, richly endowed with natural resources, with almost unlimited possibilities for growth. The labour force was, as compared with that of the United Kingdom, inadequate. Hence the invention and application of labour-saving machinery and devices of all sorts. Moreover, the American employers adopted a policy full of contrast to that ordinarily followed here. Whilst many of our employers believed that low cost and high profits depended on low wages, America strove after a large output and low labour cost, and to this end encouraged the individual workman to put forth his utmost effort. It was proved that high wages and low cost of production are compatible, and in many factories it became a rule to dispense with the services of a man who could not earn a high minimum wage. This has been justified, and presents a great contrast to our wage-cutting policy which in too many instances has resulted in either direct or indirect restriction of output. The war demand was an object lesson for our employers. A depleted labour force, assisted by unskilled men and women, worked wonders in producing a vastly increased output, encouraged by expanding wages and the determination to supply our own and our allies forces with all that was necessary to win the war. The lesson is obvious to those prepared to see it. Employers must give up wage-cutting, workers must cease to practice restriction of output, if we are to win through a very difficult condition of affairs with success.

In America the policy of encouraging a maximum output has led to what is known as scientific management. In its essence this means employing only the super-man in industry. Its results are most impressive superficially, and whilst practised on a compara-

tively small scale, it gives an impression of
soundness. If, however, this policy was to
be carried to its logical outcome, it would
stultify itself, because it would mean employing a comparatively small percentage of the
population—the super-men—and they would
eventually find themselves burdened with the
responsibility of providing for all the other
members of the nation. To some extent it
may be advisable for this country to adopt
the sounder parts of scientific management,
but there is already in this country the germ
of a policy better calculated to meet our requirements. This is a system of grading[1]
which was worked out by Mr. W. J. Davis
and Mr. Evered for the brass workers of the
Midlands. Under this policy not only super-
men, but average men and men under the
average, can be profitably employed. The
ability of each worker is graded, and he is
paid a wage commensurate with his skill and
ability. This movement is well worth in-
vestigating. During the war period it has
received a set back, but its possible advantages are such that it should receive the careful consideration of all those responsible for
the reconstruction of our industries. It would

[1] Cf. *Life of W. J. Davis*, by Dalley.

reduce the residue of unemployables to a minimum, and at the same time overcome the difficulties connected with the flat-rate—the great disadvantage connected with trade unionism.

It would be dangerous to entrust the duty of grading to employers. This danger was met in the brass workers' scheme by entrusting the grading to a joint board representing employers, the union, and technical experts. A further development might be suggested which, although perhaps somewhat Utopian for the moment, may become practical politics. This would consist of bringing about a revolution in the wages system.

Now that the organisation of labour in well-recognised unions is almost accomplished, why should not the unions receive from employers the amount due for the labour of their members ? Where this was found practicable the employers would welcome it as relieving them of much anxious and harassing work connected with the rates and insurance of each individual worker, whilst the officials of the unions receiving the amounts due to their members could work out a grading scheme based on equity and acceptable by the individual, because assessed not by any outside body but by officials responsible to the whole membership of the union.

It might be suggested that this would revive the detested gang system. But this is only a superficial view, and is really untenable. Under the gang system, a ganger agreed with an employer to find the labour to carry out some operation for an arranged price. This man was working for himself and retained all he possibly could of the agreed sum. He became in many cases a sweater of the worst description, and much hardship is said to have resulted. In the suggested arrangement, however, quite the reverse would be the case. In the first place the supply of labour would be arranged by labour's own chosen officials. These men would have no pecuniary interest in the bargain. To ensure their position they would have to satisfy the members of their union not only as to the gross amount to be received but as to its distribution. The advantages of the scheme would include the possibility of framing statistics of the exact labour cost of various operations, and there would be clearer definition as to the share of the wealth produced that went to labour. Some occupations, at any rate at first, might not appear to lend themselves to such a scheme ; but in the larger industries its application should not prove difficult, and were it successful, even those occupations which at first sight seemed least capable of accepting it might find it to their advantage to try the experiment.

The union officials would under the scheme enjoy an added dignity and responsbility. They would have a more definite status when conferring with employers, and they would become great public servants of considerable importance.

The Wages System—Some Definitions and Explanations

The wage earner is paid either by the time or by the piece. Each method has its advantages, and although payment by the piece has been severely criticised there are some occupations for which it is so admirably adapted that such disadvantages as may be brought against it are more than neutralised by advantages both to wage earner and wage payer.

Time wages are where the worker is paid at so much an hour, day or week ; piece wages are payment at so much for each article or for each operation. For instance, a hat manufacturer may either pay the labour he employs at the rate of so much for each hat or at so much per hour engaged in making hats. Human nature being what it is, a man usually makes more hats when working under a piece arrangement than if paid by the hour. It is sometimes contended, however, that piece-work leads either to the workman overstraining himself and thereby shortening his working life, or to the work being scamped owing to the desire of the man to earn a maximum. There is also a feeling, or perhaps rather more than a feeling, among workmen that the extra production resulting from piece wages keeps other men out of work. Thus trade unions as a rule view piece wages with a great amount of suspicion and dislike. On the other hand, it is contended that piece-work is more economical and tends very materially to lessen the cost of production. It saves expenses of oversight, because a man under this system works more steadily and the need for foremen is lessened. It certainly meets to some extent the objection to the flat time rate, which puts all men doing the same work, irrespective of what may be their ability, on a level as to wage earning. It may not be a very satisfactory method for overcoming this disadvantage, but until some better method is introduced its benefit cannot be denied. It may be all very well to fix a minimum wage, but to tie down all workers to that minimum is rather like fighting against nature. It must tend to increase the class of unemployables, as naturally the employer endeavours to dispense with the slowest workers, who set the pace where all receive the same rate, whatever may be their output. This problem may be looked at from another point of view. There is in every occupation the average man who possesses but a minimum of ambition. He has his standard of living, and so soon as he has earned sufficient to supply that standard he is satisfied. But the man above the average is more ambitious; he not only wishes to improve his own position but to give advantages to his children. This natural desire requires the means to carry it out. In other words, men above the average not only can earn higher wages if unrestricted, but require the extra money to carry out their plans of advancement. The man who wishes to prosper must improve himself. He can do so by attending classes, *technical* or otherwise. He requires books, instruments, and tools; all these cost money. He is entitled to demand for his work this extra amount, and it is to the interests of the community that he have it. If there were no unions there might be a system of task wages or efficiency wages whereby the extra strength or ability of a worker would win its reward. These, however, under existing conditions are not possible Thus in certain occupations piece rates tend to meet this difficulty. If labour could be graded[1] and paid according to grade there would be an efficiency wage, and this may come in due course. It has already been attempted in at least one industry. Until, however, the suggested system be applied, and whilst existing conditions continue, either the flat time rate or the piece rate must hold the field. With the time system, since all full members of a union receive the same rate of pay, the speed of production and the standard of workmanship will tend to be that of the least quick and the least skilled. An object lesson as to the effects of this can be seen in a case where men have been working at some one occupation on time rates and then a piece system is introduced. When the change is made each man can work up to his capacity, and the possibilities of the highly skilled, energetic man are revealed. The average rate of production immediately changes.

[1] Cf. p. 91.

7

As to the contention that the extra production of the more capable men tends to lessen employment, nothing could be further removed from the truth. Increased production means decreased cost, decreased cost leads to a lower selling price, lower selling price increases consumption. Decreased cost in one or two staple industries has a marked effect on employment, first of all in these industries themselves, but gradually it spreads to others and leads to increasing employment and a greater demand for labour. This can be well illustrated from ascertained facts. Some employers, even where piece rates obtain, have an idea that the lower the wage the cheaper the goods. Thus they inspect their wages books and attempt sometimes, perhaps too frequently, to cut rates. This policy is known as " speeding up." For a time it may be successful, but not for long. The workers soon realise what is coming, and their reply to the cutting of rates is " ca' canny " or restriction of output. Many of our industries in pre-war days suffered considerably from this unwise policy, initiated by the employers and causing the natural reply from labour.

This brings us to a consideration of the difference of the point of view of the employer and the seller of labour. What the employer wants in order to compete successfully in the selling markets is *low labour cost*. He should therefore give his chief attention to his cost book and not to his wages book. So long as the cost of labour for a given piece of work is low it is no concern of the employer what rate the individual worker gains. And experience warrants this assertion, that as a general rule high rates of wages lead to low labour cost. This is the secret of the policy pursued in certain American factories,[1] where men must earn a given minimum or their services are not required. On the other hand the workman's point of view is *the rate of pay*. This, though seemingly so simple, is a position that is far too little realised among our employers.

Connected with the rate of pay is the necessity to understand the difference between real and nominal wages. For instance, it is difficult to compare the position of labour in the United Kingdom and in Japan by merely quoting earnings, because the purchasing power of money is so different in the two countries. Nominal wages are the amount received. Thus an engineer may receive £4 a week, that is his nominal wage. His real

[1] Cf. p. 89.

wage depends on the purchasing power of his
£4. If living on the average costs 25 per cent
more in London than in the Black Country,
an engineer in London and one in Dudley
receiving £4 a week, although nominally
receiving the same rate, are really in a very
different position. The man in Dudley is
considerably better off. Thus in estimating
the position of labour in different countries,
or in different parts of the same country, you
must take into consideration rent and the
cost of food, clothing, and other necessaries.
The family also affect the question of real and
nominal wages. Two men living in the same
town and earning the same wages are nominally equally well off, but if one be a bachelor
and the other a married man with four or five
young children the real position of the two
men is very different.

In some industries attempts have been
made to identify the interests of the workpeople with the business in which they are
engaged. This takes two main forms. There
may be co-partnership or a bonus system—
either of these involve profit sharing.

Co-partnership has been practised with
considerable success by the London gas companies, and is found in various trades, such as
printing, boot making, lock making, and even

building. The late Sir George Livesay, of the South Metropolitan Gas Company, gave a great impulse to the movement, and a co-partnership association has been organised to do propaganda work. The late Lord Furness attempted to apply the policy to shipbuilding, but either because the scheme was ill-organised or because of union opposition it failed. Under co-partnership the usual method is for the men to receive the normal rates of wages, and at the end of each year or half year a share of the profits realised go to the co-partners either in cash, or in shares, or in both. In some cases workmen co-partners are entitled to representation on the board of directors.

Where men are thrifty and decide to save the additional earnings, these methods have much to recommend them. The interests of the workpeople are identified with the business, and thus there is a minimum of lost time and waste. Each man has a definite incentive to see that his part of the work is performed as economically as possible. There are, however, two great obstacles to the permanent success of such schemes. Where employment is of a fluctuating nature it is difficult to apply in a satisfactory manner either co-partnership or profit sharing. Whilst thrift not being a too widely practised virtue, a possible but unknown bonus, to be received at some future date, may be a snare causing much inconvenience to the individual recipient. As an illustration may be given a case where a man receives, under a profit-sharing scheme, a substantial amount during the first year. Not being thrifty, he looks on this amount as a permanent addition to his wage and arranges to live up to it. For a time all goes well, but there comes a time when the bonus is less than usual, or it is found that owing to bad times it is impossible to pay a bonus at all; then the unthrifty man feels the pinch and may find himself considerably embarrassed. The moral is that so long as men work for weekly wages the safest course is that the individual shall know what his regular wages are. A bonus may be an incentive, but its precarious nature creates difficulty.

With co-partnership there is the necessity to share losses as well as gains. Here, again, the workman is at a disadvantage, for in the majority of cases he cannot share a loss, and if his capital in the business be reduced in consequence of a lean year's working it is difficult to persuade him that he is not being exploited. Under certain circumstances either co-partnership or profit sharing may work beneficially, but up to the present there is not sufficient proof that either policy can be widely applied to the permanent advantage of the worker. Co-partnership may be a useful step towards full co-operative working, but except in special cases it is not possible to say that it can be permanently successful as a remedy to industrial friction.

The efficiency of the labour force in any community will depend on sets of conditions which affect both the individual worker and labour in the mass. The individual is affected by the conditions of his birth and upbringing. It cannot be expected that a satisfactory labour force can be reared under slum conditions. The physical, mental, and moral surroundings of the child must affect its after career. The housing, water supply, sanitary conditions, food and clothing, if below a definite minimum, must adversely affect the individual. The information derived during compulsory recruiting in this country has been of the greatest value in attracting public attention to the evils attendant on improper conditions of living. Young men who could barely pass the standards developed remarkably during a few months of good feeding, good clothing, and adequate housing, together with physical exercises and an open air life. These lessons will not be thrown away.

Education, too, affects the whole subsequent life of the youth. Under a good system of elementary education a boy begins to show his bent, and the educational ladder to the secondary school, the technical school, and the university enables the boy of brains to take his rightful place in the community as a hand or a brain worker. Then there are the moral influences affecting the youth of the community, inducing thrift, industry, temperance, integrity, and a real patriotism, i.e. the submission of self.

Labour in the mass is affected by the laws and customs of the country as to combination. Labour may be free to combine ; will it have the wisdom to combine so that combined action shall assist and not retard the commonwealth ?[1]

From the point of view of productiveness, labour in the mass is vitally affected by what is called *division of labour*.

In very early days it was realised that a division of employments was beneficial to production. Instead of each man hunting, cooking, tailoring, building, or boot making

[1] This part of the subject is dealt with in another volume in this series.

for himself, those individuals having special aptitude or training in these separate occupations gave their entire time to that one calling. Each village community thus evolved its own miller, blacksmith, carpenter, and baker. With primitive methods and tools separation of employment was possible. As methods and tools improved, a still further sub-division took place, and when steam and machinery revolutionised industry it was found that the limits to division of labour were only fixed by the extent of the market.

Adam Smith saw the great importance of this stage in industrial development, and he gave much thought and care to making the subject plain.

At the outset care must be taken to differentiate between *division of labour*, i.e. the dividing up of the making of any one commodity into a number of processes—each workman becoming very expert in one simple process, and the employing of a number of workers to produce a great result. Adam Smith's illustration of *division of labour* has become classical. He was not content to theorise, he wished to have concrete practical proof of his theory. Thus he visited a pin factory and was informed that whereas one untrained man would find it difficult to make twenty pins in a day's work, if the making of a pin was divided up into ten simple processes ten men could turn out 48,000 pins in the course of a day. Since Smith's time, division of labour has been carried considerably further. At present there are machines turning out several million pins in an hour; this shows the policy carried to its fullest extent.

Adam Smith summed up the advantages attaching to this policy. It gave the workers increased dexterity, it resulted in a great saving of time, and it led to the invention of better processes, tools, and machinery. Since Smith's day other economists have investigated the subject. John Stuart Mill saw two other advantages . There was a saving in the use of tools and there was organisation of capacity. Professor Alfred Marshall observed yet another beneficial effect, and this he termed the *interconvertibility of industries*. This last is of considerable importance at the present moment. Marshall's attention was drawn to what happened in America at the conclusion of the Civil War. The great demand for military equipment had led to the building of large factories for making special weapons and munitions. Rifles had been required in large numbers, but when the war ended the demand suddenly ceased. At one large factory, owing to the making of a rifle having been divided up into a great number of simple processes, it was found possible to convert the establishment into a sewing-machine factory without discharging a single employee. There are few things superficially less alike than a rifle and a sewing machine. Yet on investigation it will be seen that in each there is a certain amount of woodwork—in the rifle a stock, for the sewing machine a base. Then the small parts, entailing fitting with screws and small adjustments demand a similar type of workmanship. Had one man been trained to make a complete rifle it might have been difficult to turn him into a constructor of sewing machines, but since each man merely did one process—one man drilling a hole, another tapping it, a third screwing in a screw made by perhaps a dozen other men, there was but little difficulty in bringing about the change of output. It was a matter of organisation and not of technical skill.

The same process is going on in this country in many factories at the present moment. These factories were built and equipped to produce various munitions of war in great quantities. For this purpose the latest labour-saving machinery was installed, and everything was done to enable a depleted and less skilled labour force to effect an increased production. The war being over, it is necessary to convert these works to the making of commodities required for peace purposes. The process of reconstruction is going on and is not yet complete, but in one large works visited it was most interesting to see what was being accomplished. Before the war these works were engaged in manufacturing small metal goods. Many of these were cast and then trued up by hand. Now bar metal fed automatically into a foolproof machine turns out these metal fittings more accurately and considerably more economically than was done in pre-war days. The new machine equipment of this country should be a big asset in re-establishing the nation.

It has already been stated that *division of labour* should not be confused with *massing of labour*. Both produce great results, but whereas the success of the former depends on skilfully dividing up a manufacture into many separate processes, and specially training one man for one special process so that he becomes very expert in it, the latter consists in employing a great number of workers to produce a great effect. It is said that when the great Napoleon went to the château at Compiégne to spend his honeymoon he wished to give his bride a surprise. At some distance from the château rise the Beaux Monts, and between the grounds of the château and the Beaux Monts rolls the forest of Compiégne. By massing a great number of men during the first night of his stay at the château, Napoleon caused a broad roadway to be cut through the forest right up to the Beaux Monts, and when morning broke he and his bride saw a broad turfed way running from the château grounds giving a very pleasing but quite different outlook from what had existed previously. This great work was carried out in a few hours by a *massing of labour*. Massing of labour can be made to produce great results in road making and similar operations, but it is very different from division of labour.

A number of disadvantages have been alleged against division of labour. These should be carefully considered together with the alleged advantages, in order that a true view may be gained of the present industrial situation, many of the conditions of which are due to this policy. It has been contended that division of labour has had an adverse effect upon the apprenticeship system. An apprenticeship of seven years to a trade where the conditions were faithfully fulfilled on both sides turned out a craftsman of a high order. British workmen trained under this system were famed the world over. But with large scale production it became unnecessary that every worker should be so highly skilled. We cling somewhat obstinately in this country to our old methods and simple machinery, and with these a highly skilled labour force was necessary. The war opened our eyes to what could be done with labour-saving machinery and a developed system of division of labour. Unskilled women after a few weeks' training were, with the aid of new machinery, able to produce a greater output than could highly skilled men working with less capable tools. It was realised that for many occupations a long apprenticeship was a waste of time, that a shorter working day could result in greater output, and that the worker might have better conditions of work and greater leisure wherein to get recreation and cultivate the higher side of his character. Under the old conditions there must be long working hours for the individual worker in order to obtain an economic output capable of paying a living wage.

Under the new conditions costly machinery must be kept as fully employed as possible, but this could be effected by shifts of labour. A short working day for the individual worker might result in a maximum production, thereby lowering the working expenses of industry and making high wages, yet low labour cost, and so low selling prices a possibility. It is these facts that need to be realised by both employers and employed at the present moment. Low labour cost resulting in low cost of production should be the employers' concern. For the worker, shorter hours, less toilsome work, and higher wages are the great aim. The old dictum that the only way to keep profits up is by keeping wages down has ceased to hold good under modern industrial conditions, though unfortunately there are some employers who are still obsessed by this obsolete idea.

It has also been affirmed that the constant application of the attention to one minor operation tends to deaden the mental faculties. Undoubtedly, in going round the munition factories where long hours were worked under war pressure, there were few days off ; the men in many cases looked as though the monotony of the work palled on them.

Women were not similarly affected, probably because women's home duties tend to monotony. But the conditions were abnormal. Everyone was being urged to do his utmost to increase output. Under peace conditions shorter hours, for one thing, will make a great difference, and although there is still need for a great output, there will not be the same impelling force. The necessary output can be obtained without overworking or overstraining the worker. Indeed, under normal conditions it may be anticipated that work done mechanically will free the worker's mind, and he will, if of an inventive turn, think out new methods and processes for still further lightening labour and increasing production. This is said to have been the experience in America.

The most serious disadvantage alleged against the policy is that it results in the manufacturing town with all its social problems. But it must be realised that these evils are being mitigated. The industrial town, like Topsy, grew. The community suddenly awakened to the fact of its existence and of the attendant problems. For several decades attempts have been made to solve these problems, and with improved methods of transport much has already been done.

Under previous conditions labour had to live near its work. With a ten or twelve hours working day, and no electric trams or cheap train services, congestion in housing appeared to be a necessary corollary to the large factory. But with a working day of six, seven, or eight hours there is going to be a great change. Indeed, that change has more than commenced. We have model villages and garden cities. The workman may now live some miles away from his work and yet be a good time-keeper. There is less and less necessity for congested housing, and the slum tends to become the habitat of the un-employable or undesirable, and he, it is to be hoped, will be legislated out of existence eventually.

Many errors have been made by people who imagine that because some evil has existed for a few decades therefore it is permanent and unchangeable. This was the cause of the teaching of the French Phy-siocrats and Malthus on the wages question. They did not take a broad enough outlook ; their survey of social conditions was limited to the experience of the age in which they lived.

Division of labour assists large scale pro-duction, but does it lead to the elimination

8

of the comparatively small factories and works ? Theoretically it does, but in practical life there is a very interesting position. With standardisation of process and manufacture in a large factory, there goes a certain inelasticity which is not so common in a smaller business. In pre-war days America and Germany supplied many world requirements with standardised goods. Special orders came to England. The work was profitable and enabled the comparatively small factory staffs with highly skilled labour to prosper. One of the features of reconstruction, now the war is over, is that we have for war purposes adopted modern methods of production and scrapped many of our old methods. It may be predicted that the small business will continue to flourish in this country, and it is to our advantage that it should. Its greater elasticity enables us to take full advantage of unexpected demands.

Moreover, our smaller works train the men of resource and initiative required in the larger works. There is scope for both, and it may be expected that whilst there will be an increase in large scale production in this country, yet the smaller business will, at any rate for some time yet, hold its own. There are occupations that hardly lend themselves to large scale production, and many classes of repair work are more suitable to the small shop with its more primitive machinery and tools, which require greater skill and initiative to manipulate.

VI

CAPITAL—A FACTOR IN PRODUCTION

OF the three factors necessary for production, land and labour are agents, but capital is an instrument. It has to be set to work in order that it may be effective. Probably there is no term in use in everyday life as to which there is so much misconception, nor would it be easy to find a word more loosely used in ordinary conversation and in the newspapers. Thus, at the very outset of the consideration of this instrument in production, it is very necessary to get a clearly defined idea of what capital really is.

The usually accepted definition of capital is so simple that one would imagine there should be no possibility of confusion of thought or looseness of statement when using the word. Capital is wealth used in production, that is to say, it is that portion of wealth which is definitely set aside for the production of more wealth. Thus, whilst all capital is wealth, only one very definite portion of wealth should be talked about as capital. A simple illustration may help to clear up any ambiguity on the point.

Take for example the wealth of an ordinary well-to-do manufacturer. His wealth may amount to quite a considerable value, but it will not all be capital.

He will own a house, which will contain valuable furniture, possibly valuable pictures and collections of china or silver, which in terms of money would represent a large amount. But this house and its contents are not being used by the owner for the purpose of production. Hence the value represented by the house with its furniture and collections is wealth pure and simple. If, however, we were to accompany the individual in question to his factory we should there find buildings, machinery, and stock, which again would represent a considerable amount of wealth. But this part of the individual's wealth is definitely set aside for productive purposes, and is capital in the economic sense of the word. Or again, take public wealth. A municipality usually owns a more or less considerable amount of wealth. In many instances there is an art gallery and museum, the buildings and contents of which might be worth many thousands of pounds. That wealth belongs to the community, but it is not being utilised in producing commodities. It is, therefore, wealth, but not capital. In these days, however, of municipal trading it is possible to visit the gas, water, or electric light undertakings of the same municipality, and there you find considerable amounts of wealth which is being definitely utilised for the production of wealth. It thus fulfils the conditions of the definition and is in the economic sense capital. One cannot be too careful at the very outset of the study of this subject to make perfectly sure that the distinction between wealth and capital is thoroughly understood.

A superficial observer might think that by organising human labour on the land, wealth could be produced without further assistance, but the moment one begins seriously to consider the conditions of production it is realised that under modern conditions land and labour, if unassisted, would be sterile and unproductive. It might be argued by making use of the imagination that there was a time when man was not assisted by capital, but such a period could only have existed the moment man made his appearance on this planet, and could have lasted but a very short time. Primitive man, face to face with the necessity of providing even primitive forms of food and clothing, must have lived an extremely hard life. If he lived on the wild fruits of the earth he had to find them, and he had to experiment as to the wholesomeness of various fruits and roots; to procure any kind of meat food he would have to catch and kill some animal, bird, or fish, and man with merely his own hands would find it extremely difficult to catch the living creatures usually available for food. He would quickly become aware of the fact that with the aid of a stick or a stone the work of procuring meat food was greatly facilitated, but the moment man realised and acted upon this he was making use of capital. This simple illustration helps us to understand one of the great functions of capital, which is to ease the burden of labour, to make it easier for man to live, to enable him to produce to a greater advantage, to produce under better conditions and on a greater scale with less physical effort.

Thus it is practically certain that capital has been assisting man from the very earliest times. As mankind developed socially, the need for capital to assist him in the material side of life would become more and more impressed upon him. He would find that by retaining a part of the produce of the chase or by husbanding a supply of fruits he would obtain a certain amount of leisure which would enable him to consider and to plan and to invent new ways of doing things. He would find that sticks or stones of a certain shape were more suitable for certain operations, and he would also see that by improving the shape of these rude implements he was still further assisted. Improvements in weapons and tools tended still further to minimise the hardness of man's original conditions. Then, doubtless, appeared the long-headed or thrifty man who found that by the constant practice of thrift he was able to obtain accumulations of various kinds, which gave him an advantage over the less thrifty contemporary. From this there would actually evolve the separation of employment. One man was found to be cleverer in adapting wood for tools or weapons ; another man had a knack for working stones, notably flints. Eventually the man appeared who realised the possibility of utilising metals. When once a man gave his attention to the making of one group of things, or one special thing, he would quickly find that he could in a comparatively short working day make far more of this commodity than was necessary for his own use, and the advantages of the exchange of surplus products would burst upon the community.

It is difficult for us to realise the very considerable advantages connected with the development which came about with the introduction of the system of the separation of employment, the forerunner of the policy which we call division of labour.

Thus the creation of capital depends on thrift. A man produces more than he consumes and is able to enjoy and utilise the balance. In order that the thrift and abstinence of such an individual may be encouraged and rewarded two things are necessary. First of all there must be security in the possession of what has been saved, and thus arise the rights of private property on which progressive communities are founded. Then, when once a man finds himself secure in the possession of what has been saved, and discovers that he is able to save more than he is able himself to utilise in his own activities, he may receive a further reward for his thrift. For he is conferring a benefit not only on himself but on the whole community. And the society in which his life is cast realises this and permits him to lend at interest that part of his accumulated wealth which he cannot utilise himself. Other members of the community who have not sufficient capital of their own to enable them to produce to the best advantage are willing, in order to extend their operations, to give the lender of capital a certain proportion of the increased gain as a reward for the use of his capital.

A smile has sometimes been caused by a recital of what is called the cabbage-patch illustration of the advantages and reward of thrift in a fairly primitive country; but under very modern conditions it is quite possible to see the essentials of the cabbage-patch illustration in active operation.

In these days when allotments and small holdings are to be found in most parts of the country, an observer who takes the trouble can trace out for himself with very little difficulty how capital is accumulated, what it does for the individual in the first place and then for the community, and why payment for the use of capital is justifiable. If when a local authority takes over some land and divides it up for allotment purposes, observation is kept on the development of the scheme, the following course of events can very frequently be noted.

There will be two holders on the same patch

of allotment, who have just managed to obtain sufficient capital for each of them to obtain the holding and to supply themselves with simple tools and seeds. They both work hard, and during the first season they produce a crop under quite considerable difficulty. Both are hard-working men, but one happens to be rather more careful than the other. The one man uses the whole of his crop for his family. At the end of the season he has been able to live better, he has been doing healthy work; he has produced a crop which has improved the food supply of his family; they have enjoyed a more generous diet, but they have consumed all that was produced. Thus when the next season begins this man is in the same position as when he commenced, and his next season's crop, provided conditions remain fairly constant, will be practically the same as the last season's. The more thrifty man, however, has only consumed a part of what his land has produced. He has saved as much as possible and has sold it, and he utilises the money obtained to provide better tools, better seeds, and more efficient manures. As a consequence of this he faces the second season under very different circumstances. The work of cultivating the land is not nearly so heavy, thanks to better tools ; he neither works so hard nor so long, and at the end of the season, provided that other conditions remain fairly constant, he has a greatly increased production, and if he exercised the same amount of thrift he has an even larger amount of products that he can sell. Thus, season after season this man steadily improves his position, thrift giving him capital which enables him to work his land more efficiently with less labour and with greater results. This shows in a simple way the great functions of capital, which is to assist man in his work, to make life easier, and to improve conditions generally. The thrifty man is getting part of the reward of his thrift. By continuing the story it is possible to see how the full reward for his thrift can be obtained.

The first man, who has not been able to save, notices that the thrifty man's tools are not always in use. He realises that if he can have the use of them he will be able to lighten his own work. He asks the thrifty man if he is willing to lend him the tools when they are not in use. The thrifty man may say, " I am willing to lend you the tools, but since they will enable you to cultivate your land better with less exertion, part at any rate of the extra crop produced as a result of the use of my

tools ought to be given to me for their use."
Thus a bargain is struck. When the thrifty
man is able not only to improve his own
methods of cultivation by means of thrift but
to assist another man who has not been so
thrifty and the other is willing to share the
extra production with his benefactor, then the
thrifty man is obtaining a full reward for his
thrift.

It has now been shown how capital origi-
nates and how it increases. The secret of the
creation of capital is carefulness, thrift and
abstinence. An individual abstains from the
present enjoyment because he is sufficiently
long-sighted to realise that by denying himself an immediate enjoyment he may provide
for the future. When once the example had
been set, and when under an ordered government security of private possessions had been
guaranteed, the growth of wealth would proceed rapidly. The accumulations that we
are accustomed to at the present day are the
result of centuries of thrift. At first growth
was slow, but as industry and commerce
flourished and the advantages connected with
the employment of a large amount of capital
were realised, thrift was more generally practised, and the benefits to the community
became correspondingly great.

At a very early period in the world's history the advantages of owning wealth became apparent, and the money-lender began to exercise his trade. Law-givers, both religious and secular, were confronted with a new problem and were not slow in attempting to regulate this new phenomenon. Nearly every code of law contains some enactment on the subject, and it is of considerable moment that the teaching on the subject of the exaction of interest on money loans should be understood.

In the Mosaic economy there was very definite teaching on the subject. Indeed it is not the least of the claims of Moses to be ranked among the greatest prophets and most far-seeing of law-givers that his teaching differed rather considerably from that of the Greeks, and contained an exception which during both medieval and modern times has had a very considerable and unlooked for consequence. Moses enacted " Thou shalt not lend upon usury to thy brother ; usury of money, usury of victuals, usury of anything that is lent upon usury : unto the stranger thou mayest lend upon usury ; but unto thy brother thou shalt not lend upon usury." (Deut. xxiii. 19, 20.)

Thus a Jew could not lend at interest to a brother Jew, but he could to a Gentile.

In India under the Brahmanical law lending by the higher castes was restricted to this extent, that members of these castes could not lend at interest except to wicked people who were neglectful of their religious duties.

Among the Greeks, Aristotle took a stronger line, and his argument is worthy of note. In treating of loans of money Aristotle took up the position that since metal is a sterile substance and is not capable of natural increase, therefore, whilst if a man borrowed an orchard or a flock of sheep for a certain period and during that period there was a natural increase, part of it belonged to the owner and part to the borrower, with a loan of metal, there being no natural increase, there was nothing to divide, and thus it was unnatural to exact interest on money loans.

There was also this consideration in more primitive times. A man usually needed a loan of money not for commercial purposes but to tide him over a difficulty. If a wealthy person took advantage of another man's need to exact usury on a loan for such a purpose he was guilty of somewhat heartless conduct. The circumstances of course were greatly modified when with the advent of trade and commerce a loan of money might enable the trader to extend his operations and make greater profits. It is curious to note that when Europe became Christianised and the Canonists began developing the Canon law to regulate the life and conduct of Christians, they too had to consider this problem. Whether they knew their Aristotle better than their Old Testament, or whether they merely took a superficial view of the subject, their decision coincided practically with that of Aristotle, for they taught that the exaction of interest on money loans was wrong. Thus, when Europe began to settle down and industry and commerce developed, the Christian community was harassed by the Canon Law on the subject of interest. Then appeared the value of the foresight of Moses in making the exception which neither Aristotle nor the Canonists countenanced. The Jew could lend to the Gentile at interest without breaking his law. There was nothing to prevent the Christian from paying interest, and there was nothing to prevent the Jew from lending and exacting interest. Thus the Jews became the money-lenders of Europe, and developed the only profession that was open to them. The state of affairs thus inaugurated has resulted in the unique position enjoyed by the Jews in the financial world. But the Christians were not altogether happy on the subject, and they made use of various fictions to enable them to get round the strict letter of the law. For instance, in connection with the use of bills of exchange there arose the question of discount. There was in such transactions payment for the use of money, but ultimately this was allowed, the fiction being that the discount in question was a payment for services rendered, namely the transport of money from one place to another. Or, in the case of a business where one man organised, and another supplied the capital but did no active work, he was allowed to share in the profits, the fiction being that whilst money itself was sterile, money joined to human effort might be productive, and therefore the man who supplied the capital might take a share of the profits. As time went on Christians even took part in banking, and this was eventually allowed, although to all appearances both the spirit and letter of the law were broken. It was always recognised that to assist the poor was a Christian act, and therefore people blessed with this world's goods were encouraged to help the poor with money. This philanthropic work was systematised by the establishment of *montes pietatis*, religious banks. At first the well-to-do lent money to these *montes* to

9

assist the poor and needy. The poor received
loans, but had to repay them, together with
an extra payment covering the cost of running the banks. When there was not sufficient money available to supply the demand
of the poor, philanthropists were encouraged
to lend, and were paid for the use of the money
lent, the fiction being that such money was
taken from lucrative employment, and therefore the lenders were entitled to an equivalent.
When once this had been conceded it was
obvious that the flood-gates had been opened,
and ultimately it was impossible to prevent
the establishment of *montes profani*, secular
banks, run on parallel lines. At the time of
the Reformation the Canon Law on the subject still held that payment of interest on
money loans was wrong, and when Luther
was applied to on the subject he adopted the
somewhat equivocal attitude that though
theoretically the exaction of interest was
wrong, yet owing to man's fall, a useful ecclesi-
astical fiction, it should be allowed. Calvin
took up a much stronger and saner attitude
on the subject. He argued that no one denied
the right of the owner of a house to exact rent
for the use of the house, and that if that was
right it could not be wrong to pay for the use
of the money that built the house. It may

be that this common-sense teaching of Calvin had something to do with commending his views to the progressive commercial communities.

As far as this country is concerned, laws against usury existed from as early as the ninth century, but as business and commerce increased they were more honoured in the breach than in the observance. Finally, Jeremy Bentham's letters in defence of usury made plain the inconsistency of the situation, and in 1854 the remnants of this legislation disappeared.

The payment of interest on money loans is still denounced by some people, but in practice in every civilised country it is now considered lawful, and the use of capital can only be obtained on two conditions. The individual who wants to borrow capital must be trustworthy and he must pay interest for its use.

It has been already stated that capital as a factor in production is an instrument, and like all instruments it requires someone to set it to work. The person who does this is the organiser of industry. On him lies the responsibility for operating an instrument, the use of which involves more than usual risks. The instruments with which we are usually familiar may be used by even unskilful persons without any great risk of damaging them. For instance, a beginner at golf may obtain a first-class set of clubs, and he may have a very trying experience when he first essays to use them, but these same clubs in the hands of a competent player will perform their functions unimpeded by the want of skill of the previous player ; or a piano may cause extreme annoyance to those who hear it strummed on by a beginner, but if a musician seats himself at the same piano he may produce considerable pleasure. In other words, the ordinary instruments of everyday life are not necessarily damaged or deteriorated in any way by an inefficient user. But this instrument, capital, has this extraordinary characteristic that it is destroyed in the using, and thus if any organiser makes use of capital unsuccessfully the instrument has disappeared in the using and the community suffers. It is the responsibility of the organiser to so utilise capital that he not only keeps in existence a body of capital equal to the amount he is utilising in his business, but he must make additional amounts to pay the interest for the use of the capital, to repay himself for the work of organisation, and he should make a further sum in order to increase the stock of capital in existence. Progress, both commercial and social, depends on the increase of the capital available in the community.

Thus the organiser of industry is a very special and a very highly skilled worker, and as such he has to be paid. The exact nature of his reward has varied with the circumstances and conditions of industrial organisation. When industry is carried on under the system of capitalist employers, the reward of the organiser will be his profits, but during the past half century there have been developments in industrial organisation which have very materially affected the position of the organiser. Fifty years ago the reward of the organiser might quite rightly have been defined as his profits. To-day it would be more true to say that he receives wages of superintendence. Attention may be drawn to a very important Act of Parliament which was passed in the middle of last century—the Industrial and Provident Partnership Act. Prior to the passing of that Act, co-operation of either capital or labour in production or distribution was not protected by the law except in the case of certain favoured chartered corporations. By the Act just mentioned the Co-operative Societies, which had been existing under considerable difficulty for the past half century, had their position legalised, and this led to another development which can hardly have been anticipated by the advocates of the co-operative movement. About three years after the passing of the Industrial and Provident Partnership Act the first Limited Liability Act was passed, and by 1862 this new policy in industrial and commercial organisation had taken on its final form. Under limited liability a man's financial responsibility is limited (so far as the business in which he is interested may be concerned) to the nominal value of the shares he holds. This has to a great extent revolutionised the position of the organiser. The board of directors takes the place of the capitalist employer, and the advantages connected with the system have to a great extent resulted in eliminating the capitalist employer. The change should also have another marked effect ; the salaried manager of a company should be regarded as a member of the industrial army, as the highest type of skilled labour, a man capable by training and experience of operating the most delicate machinery. It cannot be too clearly understood that the labour force of the community is one and indivisible, and any suggestion that there is no identity of interest between the various grades of the industrial force should be viewed with the strongest suspicion. Indeed, it is usually the mark of an attempt to create industrial friction and cause inharmonious working amongst the factors of production. It is not usually realised that the experience required successfully to plan and equip a factory and organise it in all its departments, exercising the law of substitution whereby the right proportion of the three factors are set to work for a given object, and then the knowledge of the raw material markets, and, finally, the ability to place the finished product in either the home or the foreign markets requires a skill and an ability far in excess of that required for the working of even the most complicated piece of machinery used in the actual process of manufacture. The brain power required for this work may not be of a very high order. That is a point which is arguable. But it is of a very rare order, and as a consequence the exceptional man who can utilise capital successfully in the work of production is a man who can command exceptional terms for his services. Indeed, in these days of mass production, which involve the use of very large amounts of capital and a wide knowledge of world conditions, this type of labour is the most highly paid in the world.

The modern industrial company has to pay the factors in production. For the use of land there is rent, for the use of labour there is wages or salaries, and for the use of capital there is interest.

There is, however, another phenomenon that requires consideration. At stated periods the modern company declares dividends, and these dividends vary very greatly in amount. There are some businesses which are engaged in working new processes, or new patents which may have been developed at considerable cost, and sometimes at a very great risk of failure. If successful, these companies sometimes divide what appear to be excessive profits, but before deciding that any profit is excessive the whole of the conditions under which that profit has been earned ought to receive full and fair consideration. There are other firms which have earned a reputation, and by means of their trade marks or special brands are able to make an additional profit as a result of this well-earned reputation. Such businesses as have just been mentioned require special treatment from the economist. In this short essay attention will be limited to the dividend and profits of ordinary competitive businesses connected with staple commodities. In these the average profit made is as a rule not excessive, but as in the case of land, some of which is on the margin of cultivation and some of which, owing to its extra fertility or advantageous position, commands a greater rent, so there are manufacturers who are on the margin of production and merely make a bare living, whilst there are others who through successful organisation make comparatively great profits. The published results of limited liability companies show that some make hardly any profit, whilst others pay handsome dividends. In any one industry, indeed, there will be found a graduated scale of profits between these extremes. In an industry where labour is well organised all the firms may be making similar commodities and working with union labour, which means that the nominal wages paid are the same. It is sometimes thought that the comparatively big profits made by some companies are made either at the expense of the wage earner employed or at the expense of the consumer, but a consideration of the conditions of these industries shows that such is not the case. The large profits made in the production of ordinary staple commodities under competing conditions are the result of

9 *

successful organisation and are not due to the
manual labour employed, nor does the consumer pay for them in the price of the commodity. The demand of the market is such
that the producers on the margin, although
making but a bare living, are tempted to continue supplying it. With increasing demand
the margin tends to fall. The price of the
commodity on the market depends on the
cost of production by the marginal producer,
and it is owing to the demand for his services
that the thoroughly efficient organiser is able
to make a greater profit. When demand
decreases and the margin shrinks the profits
of the more efficient producer tend to fall.
So far as the wage-earner is concerned,
though the efficient and the less efficient
organiser may be paying the same nominal
rates, in reality the employees of the efficient
employer are usually better off than those of
the less efficient, because conditions of work
are better, and there is greater regularity in
the employment, with the result that the real
wages of the labour employed are greater.
This result leads to the conclusion that in the
interest of both worker and consumer the
object of the community should be to dis-
courage less efficient producers, and yet there
are some people who advocate limitation of

profits which, if the above argument be tenable, would only result in penalising the skilled organiser and in putting a premium on inefficiency. There has already been considerable experience of what results from the policy of limitation of profits in causing extravagance and inefficiency in management. The history of such undertakings as the Dock Companies of London, only to mention one instance, is evidence of this. The whole argument shows the necessity for entrusting the wealth of the community, which is to be dedicated to the work of production, to the most capable organiser. Capital should be in the right hands in the interests of all concerned, including both workers and consumers.

Just one word more as to profits. It is sometimes thought that the amount of dividend paid on capital invested in industry should be but little in excess of the normal market rate for money, and that any additional sum available for distribution should be devoted either to the worker or to the consumer. From the argument that has just been elaborated it will be realised that in the first place if there were no inducement to make this additional sum there might be nothing to divide between the two classes mentioned, or, indeed, that a very different result might be experienced, namely, that the discouragement of skilled management would lead to higher prices and possibly lower wages, or to inferior conditions of employment. The gross profits of a successful business should be regarded as consisting of first, the normal rate of interest on money in an absolutely safe investment, then an extra amount which would represent an insurance against risk commensurate to the risk involved in investing capital in a given business ; there should also be a further amount that would be pure economic profit, which the skilled organiser is willing to divide with those who share the responsibilities of the business with him by embarking their capital in it and as a reward for taking their part in the financial risk. If this economic profit in ordinary competing business be injudiciously interfered with the ill-effects on industry can hardly avoid being serious.

At the beginning of this section there was traced out the origin of capital, and it was shown to be due to thrift and abstinence on the part of the individual or community. The illustration made use of was that of a poor man working on an allotment. Such thrift is of the greatest value to the community, but some of the great accumulations of capita are in the hands of wealthy individuals, and it may be asked is it correct to talk about the abstinence of the wealthy man ? Indeed, it has sometimes been asserted that the wealthy man exploits the poorer members of the community and lives on their labour. This position should be considered, and an attempt should be made to estimate to what extent the community is indebted to wealthy people who invest their wealth either in State or municipal loans, or in industrial and commercial enterprises. Take as an illustration an individual who receives intimation that a wealthy relative has died and has left him a fortune—say £100,000. Under present conditions, that money becomes the property of the legatee, and it is his to do with as he likes. He may consume it entirely on his own pleasures. He can have a comfortable house, and can give himself up to a round of gaiety, with the result that his legacy may be consumed in a few years, but during that time he may have what is sometimes looked upon as a thoroughly enjoyable life. He may give himself up entirely to the selfish enjoyment of his good fortune. On the other hand, if he be a thrifty soul, he may decide to forgo the pleasure of thoroughly enjoying the whole of the legacy in a short time, and he may decide that he will invest the money and live on a comparatively small annual sum. On the advice of his stockbroker he may invest his money in a carefully selected number of industrial companies. He may get on an average eight or ten per cent for his money, and he has an annual income which, so long as these companies remain successful, is available for himself and for those who come after him. What is the result of his decision to postpone the immediate enjoyment of his legacy? The result is that the community get the advantages of this capital, and the fund available for employment is increased to that extent. He takes his risk of these companies being successful or otherwise. The successful companies do not divide up the whole of their gross profits, but they set aside annually a certain amount for keeping their plant and equipment generally efficient and up-to-date. Thus again there is abstinence. Another extra sum which might be enjoyed is deliberately set aside with the object of making the business permanent. In the first instance the individual forgoes the immediate enjoyment of a large sum, the use of this he hands over to the community, and in return he gets an annual income. Secondly, that annual income is decreased to the extent that arrangements are made for keeping the capital in the business effective. This is a justification for continuous profits or permanent interest. An individual frequently acts in this way. If the community were to take over the wealth in question, would it act with equal foresight ? Would the socialisation of capital result in the same efficiency as is the general characteristic of the present system ? Thus, the gibe that is sometimes made at what is derisively called the abstinence of the millionaire is seen to have but little foundation. The wealthy man who invests his money rightly benefits the whole community, and he has a right to expect a return for the benefits conferred.

INDEX